T4-AKL-490

writing@ online.edu

JANICE R. WALKER
Georgia Southern University

JOHN RUSZKIEWICZ
University of Texas at Austin

LONGMAN

An Imprint of Addison Wesley Longman, Inc.

New York • Reading, Massachusetts • Menlo Park, California
Harlow, England • Don Mills, Ontario • Sydney • Mexico City
Madrid • Amsterdam

Publishing Partner: Anne Elizabeth Smith
Supplements Editor: Donna Campion
Marketing Manager: Renée Ortbals
Project Manager: Bob Ginsberg
Design Manager and Text Designer: Wendy Fredericks
Cover Designer: Kay Petronio
Cover Photo: © PhotoDisc
Art Studio: ElectraGraphics, Inc.
Technical Desktop Manager: Heather A. Peres
Senior Print Buyer: Hugh Crawford
Electronic Page Makeup: Carole Desnoes
Printer and Binder: Webcrafters Inc.
Cover Printer: Webcrafters Inc.

Netscape Communicator 4.5. Copyright © 1994–1998 Netscape
Communications Corporation, all rights reserved.
Netscape Navigator Gold. Version 3.01Gold. Copyright © 1994–1996
Netscape Communications Corporation, all rights reserved.
Microsoft Internet Explorer 4.0. Copyright © 1995–1997 Microsoft
Corporation, all rights reserved.
America Online 4.0 for Windows 95 and Windows 98 Revision
135.190 (32-bit). Copyright © 1992–1998 America Online, Inc., all
rights reserved.

Library of Congress Cataloging-in-Publication Data

Walker, Janice R.
    Writing@online.edu / Janice R. Walker, John J. Ruszkiewicz.
        p. cm.
    Includes index.
    ISBN 0-321-02699-3
    1. English language—Rhetoric—Computer network resources.
2. World Wide Web (Information retrieval system) 3. Academic
writing—Computer network resources. 4. Internet (Computer
network) 5. Online data processing. I. Ruszkiewicz, John J., (date)- .
II. Title. III. Title: Writing at online.edu.
PE1408.W31319 2000
025.04—dc21   99-27392
                                                             CIP

Copyright © 2000 by Addison-Wesley Educational Publishers Inc.

All rights reserved. No part of this publication may be reproduced,
stored in a retrieval system, or transmitted, in any form or by any
means, electronic, mechanical, photocopying, recording, or
otherwise, without the prior written permission of the publisher.
Printed in the United States.

Please visit our website at http://www.awlonline.com/researchcentral

ISBN 0-321-02699-3

12345678910—WC—02010099

CONTENTS

P A R T 2
Finding Information 29

P A R T 3

Designing Your Project 83

P A R T 4
Documenting Electronic Sources 131

PREFACE

Writing@online.edu is a concise guide to finding, evaluating, and using electronically accessed sources—whether from an online library catalog or the World Wide Web. Useful for the novice researcher as well as the experienced Internet user, *Writing@online.edu* offers advice for both print and electronically published projects. Among its features are the following:

- Thorough discussions of ethics and copyright issues involved in the use of electronically accessed material
- Helpful how-to's for finding and evaluating online sources using search engines and electronic library catalogs
- Suggestions for determining the best formats for presenting a research project
- Guidelines for documenting electronic sources following MLA, APA, CMS, and CBE styles and the new COS system.

Because *Writing@online.edu* answers questions not addressed in traditional texts, it can be used as both an ancillary to writing handbooks and as a quick reference tool. It is written, however, with the assumption that the research and writing process must be approached strategically—whether research materials are printed or electronic. That is, researchers must review sources conscientiously, organize projects well, and document sources accurately. Although the tools for research and writing have changed dramatically in the past few years, the critical thinking skills required of researchers and writers are still of utmost importance. All these skills are reinforced in *Writing@online.edu*.

Similarly, ethical considerations remain an essential component of writing and research. Many researchers

are especially worried today that the availability of online sources increases the potential for plagiarism. They
are also confused by what constitutes legal use of online
material. So we begin *Writing@online.edu* with guidelines for using electronic sources or materials ethically,
approaching this issue from the perspective of current
debates over intellectual property laws. The guidelines
we present are flexible enough to allow for change as
online writing, research, and publication evolve—as
they surely will.

We also know that researchers are concerned about the
quality of materials they are finding online. Learning how
to evaluate such sources has become as important as learning how to find them. So *Writing@online.edu* offers researchers help in determining the reliability of both traditional and electronically accessed sources. The book also
suggests how to produce documents that future researchers
will be able to evaluate and document more easily.

An important feature of *Writing@online.edu* is that it
does not assume that "papers" will be produced in traditional formats. We realize that authors today may be
working with traditional texts (using electronic means),
traditional texts translated into HTML formats for online publication, or nontraditional texts that include
multimedia, active links, and other new technologies.
For that reason, we try to help writers and researchers
understand and choose the formats most appropriate to
their work. Further, we offer information to help researchers and writers formulate their own guidelines for
operating in these often quite new electronic environments.

To keep the book concise, we have not included
extensive how-to's for HTML authoring, computer use,
or other technical areas. Many good books and Web sites
offer instruction in these areas, some of which are
listed, along with documentation updates and other new
information, at http://awlonline.com/researchcentral. However, we have tried to be as specific as possible in offering
advice about research to novices and experts alike, understanding that new developments in technology will
quickly modify many of our guidelines. Rapid change is a
fact of life in research today; it is also one of its pleasures.

Acknowledgements

We are grateful for the help and support of many people in bringing *Writing@online.edu* to fruition: In particular, we would like to thank the following reviewers who have given us the benefit of their expertise: Dr. Janet Auten, American University; Lisa Carlisle, Community College of Aurora; Dr. Catherine Carr Lee, University of Texas at Dallas; Dr. Vandana Gavaskar, Ohio State University; Patricia Hofer, Glendale Community College; Robert Hogue, Youngstown State University; James R. Musgrave, Grossmont College; Dean Rehberger, Michigan State University; Colleen Schaeffer, California State University, Northridge; David Solomon, University of Connecticut; and Edward P. Tober, Jr., Tarleton State University.

We would also like to thank our online colleagues, especially those with whom we have spent hours of discussion in MOOs and listservs regarding the nature of online scholarship. The guidelines presented here grew from these conversations and thus truly represent the collaborative work of the pioneering teachers, students, publishers, scholars, and interested others who have been intimately involved in creating, critiquing, and using online spaces. We cannot hope to name them all, of course, but we have listed several useful sites of conversation in appropriate sections of the text, as well as on our Web site.

We wish to thank, too, the editorial team at Addison Wesley Longman, especially Anne E. Smith, who supported this project with all her considerable talent and energy; Rebecca Gilpin, whose indefatigable efforts and patience helped navigate this manuscript through the process of submission, review, revision, and publication; and Bob Ginsberg, who guided the book through the difficult stages of production. They helped to turn an idea into reality.

Last, but certainly not least, we would like to thank our students and our colleagues for pushing us to consider the changes prompted by new technologies that have taken place in the classroom, in the writing process, and in the research process.

Special thanks to the Information Literacy team at the University of South Florida library—Ilene Frank, Jim Vastine, Bill Patterson, and Drew Smith—as well as others who not only helped answer countless questions about the modern research process but lent their expertise to help us determine what questions needed to be asked. We also wish to thank John Slatin and Peg Syverson at the Computer Writing and Research Lab of the Division of Rhetoric and Composition at the University of Texas at Austin; their facility has helped keep us in touch with important developments in research and pedagogy.

JANICE R. WALKER
JOHN J. RUSZKIEWICZ

Getting Started

Research is a process of discovery. You do research when you look for information. Sometimes you need to find out what has already been said about a topic or to verify what is believed to be true. Just as often, you'll investigate what remains to be learned about a subject—or you'll explore entirely new concepts or find new ways to look at old ideas. In this guide, we help researchers decide where to look for information, how to use research tools, and how to evaluate the materials and information they find.

Obviously, not all methods of research produce the same results. The material you are seeking and the time you have to find it may determine where and how you look for information. For example, if you were to research what's on TV, you might either check *TV Guide* or flip through all 58 channels offered by your cable system. The two different research methods would, however, generate different types of data. *TV Guide* could provide information about particular episodes and future programs that you cannot discover through channel surfing. Alternatively, it may be more time consuming and costly to locate a *TV Guide* and the information you receive from the magazine may seem less direct than surveying programming options directly with your remote. You have to decide which tool and method best serves your research needs.

Doing serious research—whether in school or on the job—will require similar, if much more complex, choices, but you'll likely find the work exciting, challenging, and rewarding. Not only will you learn to share in the information others have discovered; you will eventually contribute ideas of your own, and that's what research is all about. As a researcher you'll especially appreciate the revolution that online research is encouraging today in almost every academic field and professional endeavor. True, electronic resources can sometimes be confusing or frustrating—downloading files can take time, Web sites are often glitteringly empty, and the quality of discussion in newsgroups and listservs may be wildly uneven. But such problems usually represent the growing pains of a new medium. In the long run, online and electronic sources will likely prove as indispensable to writers and researchers as traditional libraries. Learning to harness the power of online searches and electronic databases can help make the task of finding, evaluating, and using information and ideas much less daunting.

The word *online* itself means different things to different people. To most, it suggests being connected (usually via a modem) to the Internet or to an electronic information service such as America Online or Microsoft Network. To others, it means gaining access via a home computer to a library catalog and, perhaps, to full texts of articles from specialized databases. *Online information,* then, is any material you retrieve from a computer linked to other sources of information, whether you are using a stand-alone personal computer at home or one linked to a remote service or network.

Some of these sources have appeared previously in traditional print forms, but many now exist only in electronic formats. Even those that share formats—for example, the print and electronic versions of major daily newspapers such as *The New York Times*—feel very different when viewed in print and on screen. And some online "works" are simply hard to describe in print terms—activities such as MOOs or streaming videos. It is not surprising, then, that the newer electronic materials are raising fundamental questions about research. Because online sources do their jobs so differently, people are rethinking the relationship between "authors" and their intellectual property in ways that may eventually affect anyone involved with ideas, words, and images—which is to say, just about everyone. So we begin by exploring, if only briefly, some basic principles of research, writing, and authorship.

The Ethics of Research

Scholarly writing is an ongoing conversation. To make the thread of this conversation visible, scholars and researchers have established procedures (called *documentation*) for giving proper credit to others for their words and ideas. The conventions of documentation are both straightforward and demanding. For example, all direct quotations must be acknowledged—even one- or two-word quotations when the terms involved are significant. Paraphrases and summaries of borrowed material, too, must be credited and offered in a researcher's own voice, not simply rearranged or slightly recast from the language of the original source. Plagiarism must be avoided, even the unintentional kind that may come from sloppy note taking. The basic principle is clear: No matter where information comes from—whether television, personal conversations, books and articles in the library, or the World Wide Web (WWW)—a writer or researcher must give proper credit.

Professional considerations go beyond merely avoiding plagiarism, however; authors must also ensure that information is presented *ethically*. For example, words can be drawn out of context to make them appear to say the opposite of what they intend. Similarly, simply changing the scale of a graph can make statistical information seem more or less significant than it is. Such practices are dishonest. Similarly, ignoring information or ideas that contradict your point can also mislead the reader who relies on you. When using the words or ideas of others, you are obligated to present them as they appear in their full context, not as you would prefer to use them to support you own positions.

Presenting information without proper citation is not only unethical; it may also be illegal. You can be meticulous and thorough in your citations yet still violate copyright law. Currently, legislators and other interested parties are debating how to modify copyright legislation to reflect the changing nature of publication and communication in electronic environments. Some of their proposals threaten the ability of writers to use sources at all, regardless of how scrupulous and meticulous they may be in crediting their borrowings. To preserve access to sources in the future, it is important that writers today understand the concept of *intellectual property* (that is, the claim to ownership of ideas) and adhere to sensible and ethical guidelines in using sources, particularly electronic ones.

1.1.1   **Intellectual property rights and fair use.**   Original creations and ideas are legally protected by patents, trademarks, and copyrights. When we create an original machine or process, we *patent* it, which means we own the rights to produce the invention: we can sell (or rent) those rights to others, and we can receive compensation for such use. When we create an original work of words or art, online or in print, the same principles apply, but the protection of rights is called *copyright* instead of patent. We still own the rights to reproduce our work, we can sell (or rent) them to others, and we have the prerogative to receive compensation or recognition for such use. Patents require formal registration; copyrights do not.

According to U.S. copyright law, an author owns his or her words the minute they are "fixed in any tangible medium of expression, now known or later developed, from which they can be perceived, reproduced, or otherwise communicated, either directly or with the aid of a machine or device." Copyrighted material may be included in other works, without prior permission or payment of royalties, under the doctrine known as *fair use*.

> The fair use of a copyrighted work, including such use by reproduction in copies or phonorecords or by any other means specified . . . , for purposes such as criticism, comment, news reporting, teaching (including multiple copies for classroom use), scholarship, or research, is not an infringement of copyright. (17 USC Sec. 107)

Whether a given use is protected by this definition depends on the following considerations.

- The purpose and character of the use, including whether such use is of a commercial nature or is for nonprofit educational purposes
- The nature of the copyrighted work
- The amount and substantiality of the portion used in relation to the copyrighted work as a whole
- The effect of the use on the potential market for or value of the copyrighted work

Usually, fair use means borrowing no more than 10 percent of a work (a poem, paper, or other document) and giving an author or artist proper credit. There are various ways to give such credit. (See Part 4, "Documenting Electronic Sources.")

Using someone else's form of expression without permission, however, is plagiarism, a serious offense. Plagiarism includes failing to cite the source of any direct quotations used, as well as failing to give credit for borrowed ideas paraphrased from a source. But even beyond penalties imposed by teachers and university regulations for scholastic dishonesty, there can be legal penalties, including fines, for use of copyrighted materials without permission, *even when proper academic credit is given*.

1.1.2   Copyright and the World Wide Web.
Before computers were linked by the Internet, most college papers and projects remained within the relatively

safe legal space of the classroom. Students seldom had to worry about penalties for violation of copyright law—even when penalties for plagiarism were actively enforced on campus. Moreover, students were permitted to use copyrighted material within limits in the classroom so long as they properly cited their sources. For example, college papers and reports routinely included graphics and figures copied from published materials. However, the World Wide Web has raised new complications because students can both borrow material from the Web and publish their work there. Because the classroom is no longer restricted to a room in a campus building, authors and publishers have become concerned about what happens to their work when students use it.

Governments around the world (including our own) have yet to settle on the laws regarding copyrights, fair use, and electronic sources, but some important guidelines have evolved. You should take them seriously.

a **Always give credit where credit is due.** People deserve recognition for their ideas and inventions. So claiming credit for someone else's ideas would be unethical even without laws and teachers' red pens. But there are positive reasons to document borrowings fully.

- You thereby give credit to the originator of an idea.

- You show that you have done your research and know what you're talking about.

- You tell readers where to find your sources if they want more information.

b **Whenever possible, use primary sources.** A *primary source* is one in which the idea you are citing originated. *Secondary sources* are those in which the words or ideas of others deal with the original idea. For example, a description by an eyewitness to an event is a primary source; a newspaper account of what the eyewitness said in court is a secondary source. When you write about literature, the book or story you are analyzing is your primary source (for example, Shirley Jackson's "The Lottery"); works *about* the story are secondary sources (Jonathan Burns's "The Hidden Truth: An Analysis of Shirley Jackson's 'The Lottery'").

In a courtroom, eyewitness accounts are obviously preferred to hearsay. The same principle holds true when you are conducting research and compiling research projects. How can you be sure that a secondary source has accurately quoted, described, or interpreted an original text or idea? The answer is simple: check the original for yourself.

Of course, verifying a source is not always possible. Sometimes the original text is not available or may be difficult to access. This problem is especially acute with electronic sources; difficulties in tracking down material from electronic discussion forums, forwarded files, and disappearing Web sites sometimes make it necessary to depend on secondary sources. Your citations should always make such reliance on secondary material clear.

c   **If it's on the WWW, it's published.**   In a traditional paper handed in to an instructor, you are usually free to include graphics, pictures, quotations, and paraphrases from other sources without prior permission or payment of royalties—provided, of course, that the sources are properly cited. However, when you make documents and graphics available on the World Wide Web, you are publishing them. Your work is immediately available to anyone in the world who has electronic access, and this may affect the economic value of the source material. Why would readers buy a magazine or book if they can read substantial portions of it for free in your Internet Web project?

Of course, copyrights don't last forever. When copyrights expire, works go into the *public domain*. Many works of literature now in the public domain are available at no cost on the World Wide Web. And some newspapers and journals have chosen to make online versions of their publications available for free, though others require a subscription or payment to access them. It is important for you to know the difference between works in the public domain, which can be used without permission or payment of royalties (although it is still necessary—and ethical—to cite these sources accurately), and copyrighted materials, which can't be republished without permission.

1.1.3 **Some guidelines for the classroom.** Until authors, publishers, legislators, and international policy makers come up with more concrete regulations, the following guidelines will help you when publishing on the World Wide Web.

a **If possible, follow established conventions.** For print, the rule of thumb has been that use of 10 percent or less of a work constitutes fair use. For online sources, this same guideline seems reasonable. When you use more than this, you may need permission. For print papers that will be circulated only within a classroom, you may not need to obtain actual permission to use Web material; however, you should be aware of the steps necessary to do so and should try to locate the information required. But for work to be distributed outside the classroom—for instance, to be published on the World Wide Web itself—you must at least attempt to acquire prior permission to use material from other sources.

b **If possible, point (or link) to text files, images, and audio or video files in online projects rather than downloading them.** Some sites offer graphic images to users at no charge and may specifically request that users download them. However, other graphics and files should not be downloaded without permission; doing so violates copyright. To direct readers to such materials, you may want just to point or link to them. But even in such cases it is courteous to ask an author or site owner for permission to connect an image or file to your work, since your link may increase traffic on the server where the text is stored. Be careful of such links: files may move or change without notice or routes between sites may become jammed. (For more information on using graphics, see 3.1)

c **Always cite sources carefully, giving readers enough information to find the sources.** Document all files used in your work—including text and audio and video files. The elements of citation for electronic sources such as a Web page should include the name of the person responsible (the author, creator, or maintainer of the site); the title of the work and/or the Web site, if applicable; the date of publication or creation (if known); the electronic address, along with any directions or commands necessary to access the work; and the date on which you accessed it. It may often take a bit of detective work to locate important elements of citation for Web documents and files. But it is important to try to find as much information as possible. If some of the information is missing, include as much as you can find.

Most of the major academic styles of documentation have attempted to present guidelines for citation of electronic sources. A particularly clear and effective style, which conforms to all the major systems developed for print citation, is Columbia Online Style, presented in Section 4.1.

d **When in doubt, ask.** If it is unclear whether material on a particular Web site is available for use, simply ask the owner or author (via email), if possible, explaining the nature of the intended use and noting what portions of the work will be included in your work. If you are unable to locate information about the site owner or author, include as much information about the site as possible in your citation; you may want to add a content note explaining that the work is being used without permission of the owner, and why. If you are later asked by a copyright owner to remove material from your site, be prepared to do so promptly.

An important point here is that the WWW is an international publishing space. Many images, texts, and other files may fall under the copyright laws of other nations, whose attitude toward ownership of intellectual property may be different from our own. Thus, a key word in our own consideration of intellectual property should be *respect*, including respect for the moral and ethical as well as economic rights of authors, creators, and publishers.

Deciding Where to Look

Research is a way of finding answers to questions. You are conducting research when you look up a number in the phone book (a print source) or when you dial information to ask for the same number (a nonprint source). And, of course, you can also do research to find phone numbers on the Internet (for example, try *Yahoo*'s "people search" at http://www.yahoo.com).

Where you look for information obviously depends to a large extent on the nature of your work. Your first recourse for many projects may still be traditional references such as encyclopedias, dictionaries, indexes, and atlases, which now are available in many different formats—in print, on CD-ROM, or on the World Wide Web. You may use electronic indexes to guide you to books, journal articles, and newspaper pieces. Depending on your topic, you may use information from television programs, concerts, lectures, and even video games and software. In some situations, no existing sources or databases will have exactly the information you need, so you will have to conduct your own *field research*, using case studies, interviews, questionnaires, surveys, or personal correspondence via letters or email. In deciding where and how to search for information, you should consider three factors: the time available for your project, the availability and accessibility of resources, and the type of information you need.

1.2.1   Time.   How long you have to complete your project will often shape the kind of research you can do. For instance, you may wish to conduct surveys, interviews, or experiments to support your arguments, but you may not have time to complete all these tasks. Or if your project requires that print materials be acquired through interlibrary loan, you must be certain you have time to order and receive them. Even electronic research can be more drawn out than anticipated: networks can be slow, search engines may be frustrating, and the sheer volume of material may swamp even an experienced researcher. So begin any project with a frank assessment of time available to complete the job.

1.2.2   **Accessibility and availability.**   To conduct any research, you must have the necessary equipment and services. For printed works you need a library and its catalog (equipment) as well as an adequate collection of materials, librarians, and, perhaps, a library patron ID (services). For research in cyberspace, you need a computer and software and a modem or another connection to a network (equipment) as well as access to networks and databases or search engines (services). For most research projects, you will probably now use electronic means to access both print sources and on-line information.

For a given project, you'll likely have access to a vast range of research materials. But you may find that some sources and services are restricted. For example, a library may limit your access to items such as rare books or manuscripts, and older materials may be archived at remote locations. Fortunately, some rare sources (such as collections of Renaissance manuscripts and plays) can be examined on microfilm, and more and more scholarly materials are appearing online, including extensive collections of books (see "The On-line Books Page" at http://www.cs.cmu.edu/books.html). Indeed, your library will probably not have timely printed versions of many sources now available on the Internet, such as the latest government and congressional documents and general information about many companies and institutions, including colleges and universities. Some electronic sources may, however, require prohibitively expensive subscription fees or special hardware and software to access. Luckily, you may be able to use electronic databases such as your library catalog to locate materials at other libraries or in special collections, and many print publications now make electronic analogs available.

1.2.3   Type of information.   The type and quality of information you are seeking will also influence the scope of your search. Once again, you have many options, including the following genres of source materials.

a   Scholarly books and references.   Scholarly books and references will be among the most carefully researched, reviewed, and edited sources you will find. However, they are rarely current because they take time to prepare and publish, whether they are offered in traditional print formats or electronically on such media as CD-ROM. Scholarly books and references published on the WWW, of course, have the advantage of quicker publication schedules, although the review and editing processes will still require time.

Scholarly books make claims intended to advance knowledge in a particular field; scholarly reference works summarize what is already known or agreed on. The authors of such works are usually recognized authorities in their fields, and their claims are fully documented. Such books, thoroughly indexed, are typically written for scholarly or professional audiences and, consequently, may use highly technical language. They are often published by university presses, though trade publishers may also have lines of scholarly works.

b   Scholarly articles.   Scholarly articles (print or online) are a major vehicle by which researchers report their original findings and make their arguments. Though challenging in content and terminology, scholarly articles are essential sources for authoritative information. Like scholarly books, these articles are usually carefully refereed, reviewed, and edited for readers familiar with a given field and technical vocabulary. They scrupulously conform to style conventions (such as COS, MLA, or APA) when it comes to reporting information and documenting sources. Scholarly articles appear in professional journals such as *Journal of Counseling Psychology*, *Memory and Cognition*, and *Critical Inquiry* and in the Web versions of scholarly journals such as *Kairos*, *JAC*, or *Journal of Electronic Publishing*. Note that some journals on the WWW are the counterparts of print journals, so deciding which version to read may simply be a matter of convenience. There may be important differences between electronic and print journals, however, so you will need to cite the specific version you use.

c **Serious trade books and articles.**   These works are written for well-educated but nonexpert readers, people who wish to acquire more than general knowledge about a subject. Serious periodicals and books often report information derived from scholarly research and trace its implications. Claims are made carefully and sources are listed, but such books, essays, or electronic publications may not be fully documented. So a researcher using a serious trade book may not be able to verify all claims and supporting evidence. Works in this category, however, are often excellent sources, particularly for papers written outside your own field of expertise. Serious periodicals include magazines such as *Scientific American*, *The New York Review of Books*, *The New Republic*, *National Review*, *The New Yorker*, *The Atlantic Monthly*, and *The Humanist*. Many of these publications are available in both print and electronic formats, on CD-ROM, through information services such as America Online, or on the WWW.

d **Popular magazines and books.**   Works of this kind tend to be less demanding and shorter than serious or scholarly materials because they serve more general audiences. Popular books and magazines quite often base their claims on other, more technical sources, which may not be specifically identified or documented. Some popular magazines are designed expressly for people with specific interests, in everything from skiing to automobile repair; in these areas, they may claim a kind of expertise unavailable in other sources. Popular sources may also report events, trends, and political currents more quickly than other materials, so you can base a project on popular sources when your subject is derived from current events or popular culture. Some familiar popular magazines include *Time*, *Psychology Today*, *Natural History*, and *Smithsonian*. Many popular magazines are available in electronic versions, and some magazines such as *Slate* have been specifically created for online environments.

e **Newspapers and news organizations.** Newspapers and news sources such as CNN, MSNBC, and ClariNet provide up-to-date and generally reliable information about current events as well as features chronicling popular culture and political opinion. Usually published daily or weekly, newspapers often lack the perspective of scholarly works but play an essential documentary role. Remember, however, that most newspapers and news organizations have political biases you should consider in examining their treatment of stories and issues. Libraries often have microfilm collections and indexes of older, influential newspapers such as *The New York Times* or *The Washington Post*, and the Web sites for these newspapers may offer searchable online indexes to more current issues. Web sites sponsored by National Public Radio, CNN, and MSNBC may offer a choice of text transcripts or audio and video files of specific programs or news events that can be downloaded as well.

f **Sponsored Web sites.** Material on the WWW varies enormously in quality because anyone with access to a computer and server can post information. Many sites, however, are sponsored by trustworthy institutions, organizations, and companies, and, as a result, share the authority of their supporting institutions. Thus, Web sites posted by the U.S. government or by colleges and universities may contain reliable information. However, a university site may also sponsor student, staff, and faculty publications of varying levels of reliability. Web search engines such as *Lycos Top 5%*, *Magellan Internet Guide*, and *Excite Reviews* offer rankings of sponsored Web sites, but these rankings may be based on criteria other than those required for scholarly work. For example, although *Lycos Top 5%* reviews sites to determine whether their content is useful, accurate, and up to date, the ratings are also based on considerations such as design, amusement, personality, and charm. (For more information on Internet search engines, see Section 2.3.)

g **Business publications.** Businesses publish informational material, either in print or online, that may provide interesting material or links for a project, but you'll want to factor in the commercial intent of most such ventures. For example, a news release you find in a corporate publication will obviously reflect the interests of the company offering it. Many of these sites are useful for reference purposes, but you will need to evaluate them carefully for biases.

h **Individual Web sites and home pages.** Web sites maintained by individuals vary enormously in quality of information, design, and currency. The vitality of the Web is due in no small part to the vigorous participation of people from around the world sharing their expertise and interests. It would be folly to ignore the research potential to be found in these millions of Web pages that individuals have created on every subject imaginable. Yet caution must be exercised when relying on information from such sources. They may be updated irregularly or present unsubstantiated claims. Unlike traditional books or articles, individual Web sites are rarely refereed or reviewed by third parties who might take some responsibility for their accuracy.

One way to measure the usefulness of a Web site as a source is to consider what a reader might learn about it from a citation. A site without an author, title, date, or clear institutional affiliation leaves a reader with little information on which to base a judgment. Such sites may be invaluable for recording opinions and ideas; however, you should confirm any factual claims with information from a second, more reliable source.

i Interviews and personal correspondence.
Interviews with authorities are important sources of information. Remember, though, that an expert who is speaking or writing to you may be less precise and less accountable than the same person offering information in print. Both the answers you receive and the questions you ask in an interview must be carefully recorded. Conducting conferences and interviews online or through email aids in recording both questions and answers. Make sure, of course, that you have permission to log an online conversation (that is, to keep a written transcript of the conversation) and to use a log or an email message as a reference in your work. However, again, the nature of electronic conferencing and email means they sometimes provide less precise information than a more considered, edited work might yield.

j Listservs and newsgroups. Listservs and newsgroups enable people with specific interests to share their ideas and research. However, participants may vary widely in what they know; facts and figures may be reported unreliably or without proper documentation of sources; and the credentials of the participants may not be apparent. Anyone with access to the Internet can participate in any of the thousands of Usenet newsgroups online, and many listservs allow a wide variety of people to subscribe. As you might guess, then, these sources should be used with caution. Many listservs and newsgroups have a FAQ (frequently asked questions) posting that can provide some information about participants, along with any requirements for using information from these sources, such as whether or not you need permission from individuals to do so. You may be able to contact the list owner or moderator for more information.

Although these sites can often point you to valuable sources of information on your topic as well as help you to become familiar with issues surrounding it, you should approach listservs, newsgroups, and other such discussion forums with caution. You will usually want to verify information you obtain from these sources by checking other, more authoritative sources as well.

Evaluating Sources

Not all sources are created equal. Learning to read and evaluate your sources critically is an important part of research. Most books and journal articles have gone through a review and selection process prior to being published and especially prior to being included in a college or university library collection. However, careful consideration of published works will often reveal biases, faulty logic, or other inconsistencies. This does not mean they are not valuable resources. But you do need to learn to read with a critical eye.

As you move online, critical-reading skills are even more important. Many online sources, like their print counterparts, have gone through stringent review and selection processes. Online journals such as *Kairos* (http://english.ttu.edu/kairos/) and the *Journal of Contemporary Neurology* (http://mitpress.mit.edu/journal-home .tcl?issn=10811818) have peer review and editing processes similar to those of print journals, and many print journals such as *The Ecologist* (http://mitpress.mit.edu/ journal-home.tcl?issn=02613131) and *Computers and Composition* (http://www.cwrl.utexas.edu/~ccjrnl/) offer online versions.

However, on the WWW, it is sometimes difficult to determine what, if any, credentials a given site may have since publishing on the Web usually requires only a computer with online access and some knowledge of the necessary protocols. The same considerations hold true, then, for Internet sources as for print: read carefully, noting any questions that you may have, any doubts or ambiguities that you discover in the work. If facts and figures are presented, where did they come from? Are they the result of government or university studies? Or could they be the result of biased and incomplete samples? You are more of an authority than you may think—if the work leaves you doubting its credibility, then using it to back up your own arguments will leave your readers skeptical as well.

Evaluating Sources: Questions to Consider

AUTHORITY
- Does the author have firsthand knowledge or experience?
- Are arguments and supports presented logically and in an easy-to-follow format?
- Are facts and figures from reliable sources used to support the author's position when necessary?

TIMELINESS
- How current is the information?
- Has more recent work perhaps substantiated claims or provided more information that is pertinent?
- Are statistics or other information provided still relevant?

RELEVANCE
- Does the information answer important questions that you have raised?
- Does it support your propositions or present counter-arguments that you need to address?
- Does it present examples or illustrate important points in your project?

AUTHOR'S PURPOSE AND AUDIENCE
- Is the author's purpose apparent or explicit?
- Can you detect any biases that may affect the author's choice to present or omit facts or ideas?
- Does the author's choice of audience affect the presentation?

The checklist above offers some questions to consider in evaluating the sources you find, whether you find them online or in the library.

1.3.1   Determining the authority of your sources.   The authority of a work ultimately resides in the work itself: a work that is clearly written, easy to follow, well documented, and logically presented carries considerable weight. Is the source cited in other works? Sometimes this can be a good clue to the regard in which it is held within a field. Be careful, however; just because a work is referenced in other sources does not automatically mean it has credibility, especially if the other sources are disputing the information it contains or the claims it makes.

You can often find clues to the authority of a given source by examining elements such as its author's credentials and its publication information.

a **Author's credentials.** In examining the credentials of authors, you want to learn all you can about their personal knowledge or experience, education or expertise, and track records for producing reputable work. Books and articles often include short blurbs describing their authors, yet often, and especially for documents published online, you won't find much biographical data. Then you have to do a little detective work. Reference librarians can help, directing you to appropriate biographical dictionaries or databases. When a site includes an email address for an author, you can consider querying him or her directly.

In some cases, too, you may be able to learn about an author or the Web page sponsor by searching the domain where the work is published. For example, in Figure 1.1 (see p. 20), no author is listed for the article at http://www.public.asu.edu/~ctdiss/CAI.htm and the title bar says simply "Bonnie\web pages\CAI = Netscape." The Internet address or URL (uniform resource locator) tells us that the page is published on a university server (www.public.asu.edu); however, the next part of the URL (~ctdiss) denotes a directory that could belong to a department, a faculty member, a staff member, or a student. By moving "up" the URL from http://www.public.asu.edu/~ctdiss/CAI.htm to http://www.public.asu.edu/~ctdiss, we discover that the Web site belongs to Bonnie Kyburz and that she is a writing specialist, lecturer, and course coordinator in the English department at Arizona State University.

b **Publication information.** Publication information is also an important starting point for evaluating the credibility of both print and online sources. Publication information includes the publisher or sponsor of the site as well as the date of publication.

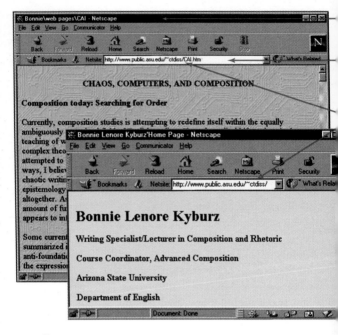

1 Title bar
2 The URL, or Internet address, for the Web page
3 Moving "up" the URL by deleting the file name

FIGURE 1.1 Determining an author's credentials. (*Source:* Bonnie Lenore Kyburz, "Chaos, Computers, and Composition," http://www.public.asu.edu/~ctdiss/CAI.htm)

PUBLISHER. A university press such as Columbia University Press or Oxford University Press will probably wield more authority than a trade press targeted toward a more popular market, such as Ballantine or Dell Paperback. Of course, this authority depends largely on your topic—sometimes the most authoritative source might be found in as unlikely a place as a comic book. The World Wide Web also has a kind of "book jacket" to guide you to appropriate sources—the domain name, usually the first part of the URL. The domain name often provides important clues to an author's location. For example, a document at http://www.cas.usf.edu re-

sides on the World Wide Web server (**www**) for the
College of Arts and Sciences (**cas**) at the University of
South Florida (**usf**), an educational institution (**edu**).
The URL breaks down into specific parts: the type of
protocol used to access the resource, the domain name,
any directories or subdirectories, the file name, and the
file extension or type. Some URLs may be missing some
or all of these parts; however, careful reading of the
URL can sometimes provide additional important information to help determine the credibility of your
source. The table below breaks down some URLs into
their component parts.

PRO-TOCOL	DOMAIN	DIRECTORY	SUBDIREC-TORIES	FILE	FILE TYPE
tp://	www.cas.usf.edu	english	walker	mla	.html
tp://	awlonline.com	englishpages			
tp://	www.whitehouse.gov	WH	html	handbook	.html
tp://	www.npr.org	programs	atc		

Generally, the last part of the domain name is also a valuable clue. A few common extensions are listed here.

.com	commercial site
.edu	educational institution
.gov	government site
.mil	military site
.net	network site
.org	an organization, usually nonprofit

Other domain names outside the United States may
be keyed to the country of origin as well as to the type of
organization. For example, http://www.unimelb.edu.au is
the World Wide Web server for the University of Mel-
bourne, an educational institution in Australia. These
are some country abbreviations you may see.

.au	Australia
.ca	Canada
.jp	Japan
.uk	United Kingdom
.nz	New Zealand

Of course, many personal home pages are found on university servers, and many commercial sites offer authoritative information. Just as with traditionally published sources, your topic and your own critical reading skills will often be your best judge.

DATE OF PUBLICATION. You will usually want the most recent sources you can find on a subject because these will reflect current trends and knowledge in the field and build on (or refute) older work. But the value of currency often depends on your subject. If you are trying to show how the sexual revolution in the 1960s changed American attitudes toward marriage and divorce, for example, you will likely want to look both at articles written in the 1960s and at later studies that examine the period more reflectively.

As you doubtless know, periodicals such as newspapers, journals, and magazines are usually more up to date than books simply because periodicals can be published more quickly. Even more current than printed magazines are news and scholarly sources on the World Wide Web. The speed of publication there is startling—work can be written and published on the same day, and news sites can be refreshed minute by minute.

But being up-to-the-minute is not always the same thing as being authoritative. For example, competition among news services to break stories first has placed more than a few embarrassingly inaccurate items in the public domain recently. And on the Internet, many sources are not clearly dated, making it difficult to determine exactly how current a site is. Moreover, many Web pages are simply left to die; forgotten and seldom visited, they become virtually worthless. So you should never rely on just one or two items for your research, whether they be printed sources or fresh off the Internet. You need to look for work that is both recent *and* trustworthy.

Determining the date of original publication or latest revision for electronically accessed sources requires some skill. Printed material from online databases or other full-text retrieval services usually includes a bibliographic record with the original publication information (see Figure 1.2). However, many electronically published articles and files may not include such data—for example, a WWW page or an article retrieved from

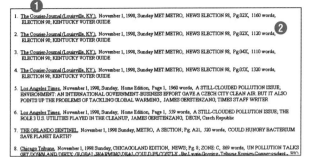

1 **Links to full-text versions of articles published online**
2 **Original print publication information is provided.**

FIGURE 1.2   An online database may furnish original publication information. (*Source:* LEXIS-NEXIS Universe, http://web.lexis-nexis.com/universe)

an FTP site. (See also Section 2.3.) Some Web pages may list the date of last modification on the document information screen, or you may be able to discover a file creation date through the FTP directory listing (see Figure 1.3). Often, however, the date you access the file is

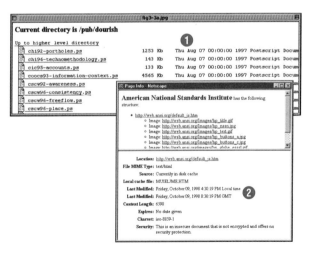

1 **A file transfer protocol (FTP) site lists date of electronic publication.**
2 **The document information screen for a Web site may provide additional information, such as the date of last modification.**

FIGURE 1.3   Finding publication information.

the only date you can offer in documenting the source. You will need to take extra care in evaluating these sources, then, to determine whether the information they present is current and reliable.

c **Primary versus secondary sources.**   A primary source is a firsthand account of an incident. Whenever possible you should include primary sources in your research. For instance, in a criminal case, the eyewitnesses represent primary sources. These might include the victims of the crime, the arresting officer, and even the person accused. However, as you well know, such testimony may be incomplete or suspect—perhaps the victims didn't get a good look at the perpetrator, or the arresting officer didn't actually see the crime. And the testimony may be biased—the alleged victims may be lying, or the suspect may tell his or her story in a way that supports a plea of innocence.

In this case, and in your own research, you should examine secondary sources that support, critique, and interrogate the testimony of eyewitnesses. You might then turn to a medical examiner's reports, the opinion of a ballistics expert, or a professional psychologist's evaluation of a victim's or perpetrator's mental state. Each of these accounts illuminates part of the original tale, just as most secondary sources comment on and extend what we know about a primary source.

When you write about a work of literature, the work itself is your primary source, and many of your arguments will be supported by quotations and summaries from the text itself. However, you also want to look at what other readers and researchers have said about a novel, play, or poem. For example, you might consult the introduction to a work in an anthology to gather important biographical information about the author or historical information about the period that lends credence to your thesis. Critical articles in literary journals and book reviews are similarly important sources of information.

Such secondary sources often give you a sense of the conversation that surrounds a primary work. Sometimes such discussions have been going on for generations; by examining bibliographies included in a work by the author, you can often get a sense of this talk. This is also why it is essential to look at several different sources on any topic to determine what has already been said and what the prevailing agreements and disagreements might entail.

If traditional scholarly writing can be regarded as dialogue, then electronic discussions are even more conversational; documents on the WWW often include links to other related sites, in essence making them, too, part of that conversation. Listservs, chat rooms, and synchronous communications are self-evidently conversational. (See Sections 2.3 and 2.4 for more about online communication.)

1.3.2 **Developing critical reading skills.** You will often need to read closely and critically to ensure that sources actually are relevant to your topic. You will also want to determine exactly how the purpose and audience of a source may be shaping the information it presents.

a **Relevance.** There is no magic formula to determine how relevant a given source will be to your topic. The best arbiter will be your own judgment: you are conducting research to find answers to particular questions and to gather support for a thesis. Each source you investigate should add something to what you know and help build your case. But not infrequently, sources will complicate your thesis or perhaps even undermine it completely. Ethics dictate that you both include and acknowledge such material in your work. In many cases, such highly relevant documents will provide a new direction for your project. Do not, however, include sources in your project simply because the information in them is interesting or just to pad your bibliography. Above all, do not let your sources or existing work dictate your research agenda. There is no point in assembling a project that merely summarizes the research others have done already.

One advantage of conducting research online is that you may find sources not available in library collections, giving your work a fresh perspective. Often these sources reflect points of view—political, social, economic, philosophical—that need to be considered, whether or not they are recognized as fully "authoritative." Note, too, that if a Web search of your topic returns many sites that provide biased information, you might in your project need to anticipate or counter misinformation widely disseminated in the popular press.

b **Purpose and audience.**   During your research, you will likely read many sources on your topic, some of which will arrive at distinctly different conclusions. You will discover that even cold facts and hard figures can be interpreted in various ways. That is because authors do not write in a vacuum; we all come to our work with biases, preconceptions, and agendas. So an author's purpose and audience do much to determine everything from emphasis and organization to format and word choice. Sometimes an author's bias or purpose is explicit—the thesis statement clearly defines what the author wants to prove and from what point of view. At other times, only careful reading will lead you to uncover the author's intentions.

Understanding an author's choice of audience can also be a key to discerning biases. A scholar hoping to place an article in a professional journal likely shares at least some of the values held by the readers in that field. Similarly, an author who decides to locate a work on the WWW rather than offering it in print decides to address a different kind of reader—one who can be assumed, for example, to have some knowledge of computers. A student decrying a proposed tuition increase might use statistics more casually in an editorial for a student newspaper than in a formal letter to the university's board of trustees. Biases in a source are not necessarily bad, but you do need to consider them in determining the value and credibility of the material.

c **Logic.**   Most writers and readers appreciate information that is presented logically, in a well-ordered, fully documented format. That's one reason why articles in professional journals can be so valuable to researchers: such articles ordinarily meet clear professional standards, right down to their punctuation. Electronic sources should be held to similarly high standards: for example, links in World Wide Web documents should be easy to follow; navigational aids and transitional statements should guide readers through arguments; and sources should be documented so that users can verify the claims presented or find additional information. (For more on logic, see "Logic in Argumentative Writing" at Purdue University's Online Writing Lab site, http://owl.english.purdue.edu/Files/123.html.)

Finding
Information

The type of information you need for a project will determine where you begin your search (see Section 1.2). For most academic work, research still begins at a library catalog. You might then expand your inquiry to include electronic databases available through your library, either online or on CD-ROM. These sources and a great many others may also be available on the Internet or through a commercial online service such as America Online or CompuServe. After you decide where to look—library, databases, or Internet—the information in Sections 2.2 through 2.5 will help you locate and keep track of specific information.

The box below lists some of the major sites and protocols for accessing online information. Electronic access to sources makes it easier than ever to find information. You can still locate material by author, title, or subject, of course, but you can also search for key words or phrases within documents—an extraordinary capability that enables you to zoom in on precisely the material you need. Online search engines can scan sources very quickly, too, examining thousands of files in a few seconds. This quick search capacity often turns up more information than a researcher can profitably review within the time available, posing a new dilemma: with so many sources to choose from, how do you decide which to use? Sections 2.1 through 2.5 suggest some strategies for managing the glut, including how to use Boolean operators to limit your searches, how to evaluate the results of an electronic search before you seek the material itself, and how to keep track of what you find.

Where to Find Information Online

LIBRARY CATALOGS
Many libraries offer access to electronic catalogs either in the library itself or sometimes via remote access using your personal computer and a modem.

THE WORLD WIDE WEB
The World Wide Web offers access to many types of information, including many library databases, magazines, newspapers, scholarly journals, personal and business sites, and much, much more.

TELNET
Telnet protocols allow the user to log on to a remote computer and access its files and programs. Most MOOs and MUDs are accessed using telnet protocols, and many library catalogs may be accessible this way.

FTP
File transfer protocol is a means of moving files from place to place, for instance, from a remote site on the Internet to your home computer.

GOPHER
This is an older menu-driven means of accessing and re-trieving information and files on the Internet.

IRC
Internet Relay Chat allows multiple users to log on to a site and communicate with others around the world in real time. IRC sites are usually organized using *channels* or chat rooms, in which conversations center on specific topics of interest to users.

EMAIL
Electronic mail is a form of asynchronous communication that allows users to send and receive messages on their computers through an online service or network. Email also allows users to subscribe to listservs, or online dis-cussion groups, which center on topics of interest to sub-scribers and automatically route messages to all mem-bers.

MOOS AND MUDS
Real-time synchronous communication sites on the Inter-net that allow multiple users to log on and "talk" to each other, usually by inputting commands on a keyboard. These sites are often used for conferences and class dis-cussions; users do not need to be physically present in the same location to participate.

NEWSGROUPS
Similar to listservs, newsgroups use email to discuss vari-ous topics of interest. Unlike listservs, however, readers do not need to subscribe. Topics cover a broad range of interests and subjects, and participants may number in the millions.

INFORMATION SERVICES
Online information is available in a broad range of for-mats from many different providers. The Internet is only one means of accessing information; services such as America Online and Microsoft Network, which charge a fee for subscription, allow access to various references, publications, and conversations that might not be avail-able elsewhere. In addition, many of these services offer access to the Internet.

Getting Connected

Before you can access information online, you need to have the proper equipment and programs, configured correctly for the type of account you have. The box below explains the basic equipment, programs, and service necessary to connect to most remote sites.

Connecting to Information Online

In order to access information online, you will need certain hardware and software.

A COMPUTER
Almost any type of computer will do. The Internet allows for transfer of information across platforms in most instances, so whether you are using a DOS or Windows personal computer or a Macintosh computer, you can still have access to most of the information. Some applications, however, require faster processing speeds, additional RAM (random-access memory), or multimedia devices.

A MODEM
A device that allows digital communication from a computer to be transmitted over ordinary telephone lines. Most graphical browsers and many client programs require modem speeds of at least 14.4 kbps (kilobytes per second). For ultimate performance, however, you will want the fastest modem you can afford.

A TELEPHONE
Unless you are directly connected to the server using cables or other types of network connections, you will need to have a telephone line in order to use your modem and dial in to a service provider. You can use regular voice telephone lines with a modem. Faster services may use special data lines or direct cable connections.

COMMUNICATIONS SOFTWARE
Some type of software is required to direct your computer to use the necessary protocols to connect to and

---

communicate with remote computers on a network. Most newer computers and/or modems come with the necessary software installed; your service provider may offer special software.

A SERVICE PROVIDER
Many services offer accounts that allow users to dial in and access information and other services on their host computer. An Internet service provider (or ISP) allows users to connect to the Internet; an information service provider allows users to access information on their computers as well as sometimes offering a gateway to the Internet; bulletin board services (BBSs) also offer varying levels of online services, such as email between members and sometimes access to Bitnet or Usenet newsgroups or other Internet sites.

Depending on your hardware and choice of service provider, you will probably have either a shell account or a PPP account. A shell account requires users to enter commands at a prompt to access files and programs that reside on the server. UNIX, VAX, and VMS operating systems are often used for shell accounts. You may need to check with your systems administrator for help with commands.

Most Internet service providers (or ISPs) now use point-to-point protocols (PPP), which allow a user to connect to the system using client programs, or programs that reside on the user's own computer. PPP connections also allow the use of offline mail editors, graphical browsers (such as Netscape *Navigator* or *Internet Explorer*), and other programs that use a point-and-click interface. Commercial services such as America Online or Microsoft Network may require that you install software specifically configured to communicate with their server. They may also offer additional resources, such as access to news services, chat rooms, or online reference materials, that are not available to nonsubscribers.

Many colleges and universities offer students free access to electronic library catalogs and resources and to the Internet. Check with your school for information on what you need to connect to these services if they are available. Many schools also provide introductory courses or tutorials and/or printed handouts to help you find your way around.

The Electronic Library

For most research projects, you will probably want to begin your search in the library. Many library catalogs, such as the one illustrated in Figure 2.1 from the University of South Florida, can be accessed and searched in the library or from home and either in a text-only format or on the World Wide Web. Such electronic access speeds your research, freeing more time for thinking and writing about what you've discovered.

2.2.1   **The library catalog.**   A library catalog typically lists holdings by author, title, and subject. If you know the title or author of a work, a catalog can tell you whether the library owns the item and, if so, where to locate it in the stacks. If the library catalog is electronic (as most now are), you can also determine immediately whether a document is checked out, lost, or otherwise unavailable, thus saving you much time.

You can also search library catalogs by subject area. Most libraries use the Library of Congress classification system to organize their collections. Works are assigned letters to designate their content or concern.

Library of Congress Classification System

A	General Works
B	Philosophy, Psychology, Religion
C–F	History
G	Geography, Anthropology
H	Social Sciences, Business
J	Political Science

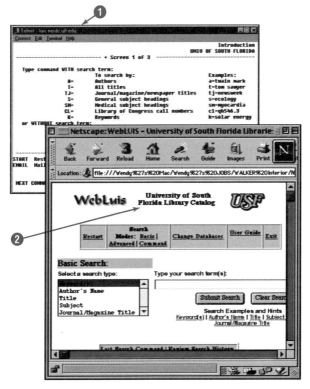

❶ Many library catalogs can be accessed remotely in a text-only format using telnet protocols.

❷ Many library catalogs can be accessed on the WWW using browsers such as Netscape *Navigator.*

FIGURE 2.1   Electronic library catalogs can often be accessed remotely. (*Source:* University of South Florida library catalog, http://www.lib.usf.edu)

K	U.S. Law
L	Education
M	Music
N	Fine Arts
P	Language and Literature
Q	Math, Science
R	Medicine
S	Agriculture

T	Technology, Engineering
U	Military Science
V	Naval Science
Z	Bibliography, Library Science

Many online catalogs also list subtopics under each major category. (Figure 2.2, for example, shows some possible subtopics under "poetry.") Such subheadings can help narrow your searches or suggest additional areas for you to explore. In addition, most electronic catalogs also support searches that use keywords and Boolean operators—more tools for locating the exact information you need.

a Keyword searching. Keywords are specific terms or combinations of words that you can direct a computer to find in documents, document titles, or key-

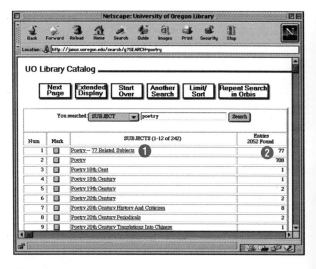

1 Subheadings under a subject may help you narrow your search or suggest additional areas for you to explore.

2 The number of items available under a subject can help you determine whether sufficient resources are available for a topic.

FIGURE 2.2 Library of Congress subject searches. (*Source:* University of Oregon online library catalog, http://janus.uoregon.edu/screens/opacmenu.html)

word lists that have been placed in a database. Because a keyword search delves more deeply and finely into documents, it will ordinarily uncover more information on a topic than a subject search. A subject search returns only sources in which a given topic is the main focus. A keyword search also turns up sources in which the topic is mentioned, even though it may not be the chief focus of the piece; thus, a keyword search provides a potentially richer range of source material. Figure 2.3 shows the results of a keyword search for the phrase "black American poetry." It includes items that would probably not be found using a subject search alone, for example, *Black Chant: Languages of African-American Postmodernism* and *Million Man March, Day of Absence: A Commemorative Anthology.*

b   **Boolean operators.**   Most online catalogs allow you to use Boolean operators that can further help to refine your search by allowing you to include or exclude search terms or combine them to search for phrases in a file or document.

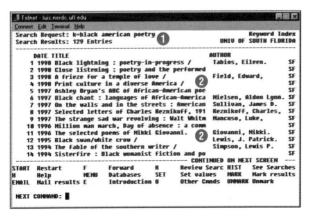

❶ You can narrow and refine a search by combining search terms.
❷ Keyword searches can find sources that might not be found using the Library of Congress subject headings.

FIGURE 2.3   **Keyword searches can help you find additional sources or narrow and refine your search.**

Boolean Operators

Term   *Description*

AND   Limits your search to only those documents that contain both terms, in any order: death AND penalty

OR   Searches for all instances of either term in documents: death OR penalty

NOT   Eliminates terms from your search so that documents containing the term will not be listed: death AND penalty NOT animals

" "   Groups words together and searches for them as phrases in a document: "death penalty"

ADJ   Finds keywords or phrases located adjacent to each other in a document or file: "death penalty" ADJ "Wisconsin"

[ ]   Allows users to nest search terms, that is, to combine groups of words or phrases and Boolean operators together: ["death penalty" AND "Supreme Court"] NOT animals

Use Booleon operators with care. Excluding terms can sometimes limit the information you find, causing you to miss important information. Alternatively, including too many terms can make it more difficult to find anything that is truly useful. Your library catalog may use variations of these terms. Be certain to read any instructions, menu items, or help files that may be available.

2.2.2 **Electronic indexes and databases.** Library catalogs usually don't help you locate material in professional journals, magazines, and newspapers. To search these essential media, you'll have to rely on indexes and databases. Fortunately, indexes cover almost every academic subject. Because of their speed and efficiency, electronic databases are quickly replacing printed volumes. Though many of these services require a paid subscription, your library probably subscribes to many indexes and may provide free access to patrons.

Most of these databases allow for searches by author, title, subject area, or keyword, and many also use Boolean operators to help limit your searches. (See Section 2.2.1). Figure 2.4 shows the results of a simple keyword search in the *WorldCat* online database. The list provides essential information about each entry, including the title, the year of publication, and the name of the author, if applicable. Reviewing such information is an important first step in narrowing the focus of your search. For example, the title can give you some idea of whether the content of an article will be useful, even before you read the article itself. Similarly, if you are looking only for more recent information, the dates of publication will help you eliminate some sources.

Some databases, such as *ERIC*, may also provide abstracts of articles, along with full bibliographic records for each entry (see Figure 2.5). The screen may also enable you to access other information, such as a listing of libraries that own a particular source, options for obtaining the source via fax or email, or links to view the document on the WWW if applicable. You can also

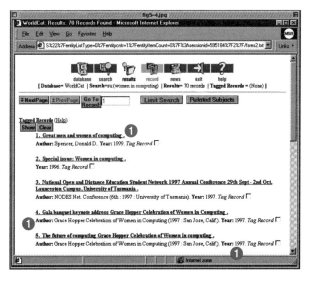

❶ **Many databases include information such as the title, year of publication, or name of the author.**

FIGURE 2.4   Database searches may give you information about sources. (*Source:* **Online Computer Library Center** *WorldCat* **database, http://www.oclc.org**)

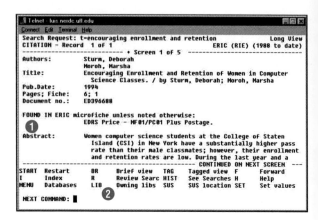

① Abstracts can help you determine whether a source will be useful before you spend time accessing the source itself.

② Many databases will help you locate the material. If it is not available in your library, you may be able to order the source through a free interlibrary loan service.

FIGURE 2.5   Abstracts help to determine how useful a source may be. (*Source:* Educational Resources Information Center (ERIC), http://www.accesseric.org:81/)

email the bibliographic record to yourself (or to someone else) to review later.

Following is a list of just a few indexes and databases that you may already have access to through your library's online catalog. Some of these indexes are also available in print or on CD-ROM. Check with your reference librarian for more information.

Electronic Databases

ABI/INFORM

Citations on business and management topics from 1,000 U.S. and international publications, many available in full text.

Anthropological Literature

Listing of articles and essays in anthropology and archaeology.

BioDigest

Full-length digest covering environmental science, medicine, health, zoology, botany, and many other categories abstracted from more than 300 journals.

Book Review Digest
Digest of book reviews in periodicals published in the United States, Canada, and Great Britain, covering more than 7,000 adult and children's books each year.

Business Index
Index of business- and management-related articles from more than 3,000 publications, including abstracts from many journals.

CARL/Uncover
Database of current articles from more than 15,000 multidisciplinary journals.

Consumer Index
Index of consumer and health-related topics from more than 100 periodicals and government resources, including evaluations, descriptions, recalls, and warnings.

Dissertation Abstracts
Abstracts and bibliographical information for doctoral dissertations and master's theses from universities in North America and Europe.

EconLIT
Subject indexing and abstracts from more than 400 journals, 500 collective volumes per year, plus books, dissertations, and working papers.

Education Abstracts
Abstracts of articles from English-language periodicals and yearbooks.

ERIC
Index of education journals and research reports covering the entire range of education topics, from preschool to higher and adult education.

FactSearch
Facts and statistics about current social, economic, environmental, and political issues.

General Science Abstracts
Covers astronomy, biology, botany, chemistry, earth science, environmental issues, mathematics, medicine, physics, and zoology.

Humanities Abstracts
Abstracts of articles in archaeology, art, classics, film, folklore, journalism, linguistics, music, the performing arts, philosophy, religion, world history, and world literature.

International Index to Music Periodicals
Index of more than three hundred international music periodicals from more than 20 countries, including articles and obituaries from *The New York Times* and *The Washington Post*.

Legal Periodicals Index
Articles from journals, yearbooks, institutes, bar associations, law reviews, and university publications, covering various legal areas: antitrust, banking, bankruptcy, commercial, criminal, environmental, estate, international, labor, landlord/tenant, malpractice, multinational corporations, real property, securities, and taxation.

LEXIS-NEXIS Universe
Access to full-text articles or abstracts of electronic sources of news and legal and business information from newspapers, magazines, and government documents; state and federal laws and regulations; case law; newsletters; and company and industry information.

MathSCI
Database covering mathematics and mathematically related research in statistics, computer science, physics, operations research, engineering, and biology.

MLA Bibliography
Covers literature, languages, linguistics, and folklore from more than 4,000 journals and books published worldwide.

NetFirst
Abstracts of Internet resources including WWW and Gopher sites, listservs, Usenet groups, and electronic journals.

Newspaper Abstracts
Indexes and abstracts from 25 national and regional newspapers, including articles, reviews, editorials, commentaries, and editorial cartoons.

Reader's Guide Abstracts
Abstracts of articles on education, current events and news, fine arts, fashion, business, sports, health and nutrition, consumer affairs, and other subjects from popular periodicals published in the United States and Canada.

WorldCat
Citations of books, computer data files, computer programs, films, journals, magazine and manuscript titles, maps, musical scores, newspaper titles, slides, sound recordings, and videotapes.

Zoological Record
References from more than 6,000 international journals, annuals, monographs, meeting proceedings, and books in the field of zoology.

2.2.3   **Reference works online.**   Dictionaries, encyclopedias, atlases, and other reference works can be good starting points for many research projects. These resources may be housed in the reference section of your library in print or CD-ROM form, or they may be available online via the WWW. Some Web versions may require access through your library server or a paid subscription; others are available to anyone on the Internet. Commercial providers such as America Online also offer their subscribers many online reference works (see p. 76).

Reference Works

American School Directory	http://www.asd.com/
Bartlett's Familiar Quotations	http://www.columbia.edu/acis/bartleby/bartlett/
CIA World Fact Book	http://www.odci.gov/cia/publications/nsolo/wfb-all.htm
Electronic Statistical Textbook	http://www.statsoft.com/textbook/stathome.html
Encyclopaedia Britannica Online	http://www.eb.com:180/

IEEE Standards Library	http://standards.ieee.org/reading/index.html
Occupational Outlook Handbook	http://stats.bls.gov/ocohome.htm
Perry-Castañeda Map Collection	http://www.lib.utexas.edu/Libs/PCL/Map_collection/Map_collection.html
Statistical Abstract of the United States	http://www.census.gov/prod/2/gen/96statab/96statab.html
U.S. Code	http://law.house.gov/usc.htm
WWWebster's Dictionary	http://www.m-w.com/dictionary

Some libraries also offer online or CD-ROM access to subscription-only reference works, such as the *Oxford English Dictionary* or the *World Almanac*. Check with your reference librarian for more information.

The Internet

The Internet is a vast network of computers from around the world that began as a medium for communication by the U.S. Department of Defense during the 1960s. More recently, it has become a civilian resource, thanks to user-friendly software that has given anyone with a personal computer and a modem remarkably smooth access to the network. Many colleges and universities now offer Internet accounts to students and faculty, while commercial Internet service providers have dropped rates drastically as a result of competition, bringing millions more people online.

Some online services even offer free email or Web space, and free chat rooms have become popular places to "talk" with people from around the world. Even people who cannot afford their own computers or Internet accounts often can gain access at libraries, schools, and community centers or even cybercafés where patrons can browse the World Wide Web.

Thanks to the Internet, students at smaller colleges and universities are no longer limited to the information and texts they can access in their own libraries. While interlibrary loan programs have long allowed most college students to arrange to borrow books from other institutions, the Internet is often a quicker way to search library databases from around the world to locate these sources. Moreover, it is the goal of Project Gutenberg, the Library of Congress, and many other sites to put entire texts online. These are usually works in the public domain—that is, works whose copyrights have expired. For example, you can read the complete works of Shakespeare on your home computer—as well as a wide selection of novels, poems, and works of nonfiction.

In addition, many magazines, newspapers, and scholarly journals are now publishing online, some for free, others for a subscription fee that is usually less than you would pay for paper copies of the same material. Some book publishers are producing Web versions of new books, including textbooks, which will allow for more frequent updates and, possibly, lower costs. And some universities are beginning to allow, or even require, electronic versions of theses and dissertations.

Also moving online are businesses, educational institutions, government agencies, nonprofit organizations, and individuals. Email and real-time communication sites are changing the way we communicate, just as the WWW is changing the way we do research, the way we write, and the way we access the work of others.

2.3.1   The World Wide Web (WWW).   The World Wide Web is a means of organizing and displaying information on the Internet. The Web supports and provides hypertext links between text documents, graphics, audio files, and video files (see Section 3.4). To access information on the Web, you need some type of browser, either a text-only browser such as *Lynx* or a graphical browser such as Netscape *Navigator* or *Internet Explorer*. Some applications may also require special plug-ins, or software that allows your browser to recognize and display specific types of files, such as files created using portable document format (PDF) or certain

---

How to Connect to the World Wide Web

SHELL ACCOUNT

Shell accounts often provide users access to the WWW using text-only browsers (that is, graphics, audio, or video files will not be readable in the browser, although it may be possible to download these files to read in software programs offline. Commands vary, but common commands to access the WWW include these.

> lynx
> www
> web

Check with your service provider or systems administrator for more information.

PPP ACCOUNT

After connecting to your service provider, you can open a browser installed on your computer, such as Netscape *Navigator* or *Internet Explorer*. Some service providers, such as America Online, may require installation of special communications software and browsers; you may be able to connect and download the software. Many companies offer free software to students.

---

audio or video files. Many plug-ins are available for free downloading from the Internet.

The Internet consists of much more than just the WWW, of course, but its ease of navigation has made the Web a primary site for publishing and research in recent years, a trend likely to continue. But with so much information available, finding what you need quickly and efficiently can be challenging. Of course, you *can* merely surf the Web at random, clicking on interesting links. With a little luck, you *might* stumble on some that are useful. Fortunately, however, tools such as directories and search engines have been developed to make seeking information online more productive.

Many WWW sites themselves provide good starting points for research. (Some of these electronic centers and libraries are listed in the box on p. 47.) Scholarly journals, online newspapers and news services, and searchable online databases also make the WWW a

Quick Starting Points—
Libraries and Text Centers

ELECTRONIC TEXT CENTER AT THE UNIVERSITY OF VIRGINIA
http://etext.lib.virginia.edu/
An electronic archive offering access to thousands of electronic texts

THE ENGLISH SERVER AT CARNEGIE MELLON UNIVERSITY
http://english-server.hss.cmu.edu/
Offers more than 18,000 electronic texts covering a wide range of interests

INTERNET PUBLIC LIBRARY
http://www.ipl.org/ref/
A ready-reference collection with a searchable database and reference librarians to answer individual questions

LIBRARY OF CONGRESS
http://www.loc.gov/
A searchable database of holdings in the U.S. Library of Congress

PROJECT BARTLEBY
http://www.columbia.edn/acis/bartleby/
A searchable site including electronic texts, bibliographic records, first-line indexing, and more

PROJECT GUTENBERG
http://www.promo.net/pg/
A collection of electronically available texts, most in the public domain, in a choice of formats

U.S. GOVERNMENT PRINTING OFFICE
http://www.access.gpo.gov:80/aboutgpo/index.html
Offers publications free or at low cost on a wide variety of subjects of interest to scholars and to the general public

WWW VIRTUAL LIBRARY
http://vlib.stanford.edu/Overview.html
A searchable collection of links to information sources, library databases, and other links throughout the world on a wide variety of topics

YAHOO'S ACADEMIC LIBRARIES LIST
http://www.yahoo.com/Reference/Libraries/Academic_Libraries/
An alphabetical list of links to college and university libraries online

rich source of information. Though much of this information may also be available in print, you are likely to find the electronic versions easier to access (on your home computer, for instance), quicker to search, and cheaper.

a **Search engines and directories.**   Probably the best way to begin your search for information online is to use one of the many Internet search engines or directories available on the WWW. Different search engines check different types of sources and may use different tools to limit searches. You should become familiar with some of the major search engines and how they work.

Use search engines such as *AltaVista* to find particular documents or files. Others, such as *Yahoo!*, include directories to help you discover information available in broader subject areas. Some search engines, such as *Excite*, offer "More like this" links to assist your inquiry or may even suggest additional keywords. Other search engines, such as *Argos*, are discipline specific, probing only sites that have been registered or evaluated. Some popular search engines and indexes are listed below.

AltaVista	http://www.altavista.com/
AOL NetFind	http://www.aol.com/netfind/
Argos	http://argos.evansville.edu/
Deja.com	http://www.deja.com/
Excite	http://www.excite.com/
HotBot	http://www.hotbot.com/index.html
Infoseek	http://www.infoseek.com/
Lycos	http://www.lycos.com/
Magellan	http://www.mckinley.com/
Snap	http://www.snap.com
Tile.Net	http://tile.net/
WebCrawler	http://www.webcrawler.com/
Yahoo!	http://www.yahoo.com

Some sites offer the option of working through several different search engines from a single location.

All-in-One	http://www.allonesearch.com
Dogpile	http://www.dogpile.com
MetaCrawler	http://www.go2net.com/
Net Search	http://home.netscape.com/escapes/search/

Search engines and directories usually provide a form or space to input simple keywords, Boolean search phrases (see Section 2.2), or plain English queries. For example, AltaVista allows you to ask a question in plain English, such as "Where can I find information on black holes?" It also offers an index of categories, including a Reference Desk with links to online dictionaries, encyclopedias, atlases, museums, and other reference sites. In addition to keyword searches, Yahoo! offers an index of sites that can be searched by following directories to ever-more specific information, as well as links to such information as the Yellow Pages, People Search, maps, and more. HotBot uses pull-down menus to allow for searching by keyword(s), phrases, or Boolean operators, as well as allowing you to limit results to specific languages, dates, types of media (e.g., pages that contain graphics, audio, or video files), domain types, countries, or other options. Netscape's *Communicator* offers "Smart Browsing," a feature that allows the user to input keywords rather than a URL directly into the location bar. The "What's Related" button can also help to locate sites with similar topics.

Several programs are also available (usually for a fee) that offer to conduct searches for you even while you sleep, such as Symantec's *Internet FastFind*. While these tools can be useful, they can also be daunting, and they will quickly fill up limited resource space on your home computer. However, they can be helpful when you need to search for a large amount of information in a limited time.

b **Evaluating your results.**   What will you get from an Internet search? You'll typically receive a list of documents or files that contain the word or phrase that you entered in a search screen. Figure 2.6 shows a partial listing of results found using the search engine *WebCrawler* for the term "black hole."

Most search engines offer to display summaries of the sites they have found in addition to links. Such summaries are often too cryptic to tell you much about the content of the site—usually they list nothing more than the first few lines on a Web page. However, the title and summary information together can often help you decide which sites deserve closer attention. The percentage shown to the left of each title in Figure 2.6 indicates its degree of reliability, which measures the number of times the search terms appear in a given Web file. When the URL for an item isn't listed, pointing to the item with your cursor will bring it up in many Web browsers. Analyzing the URL carefully (see Section 1.3) can also help you determine the authority of a site. In addition, some search engines furnish information for each item found, including the file size, the date

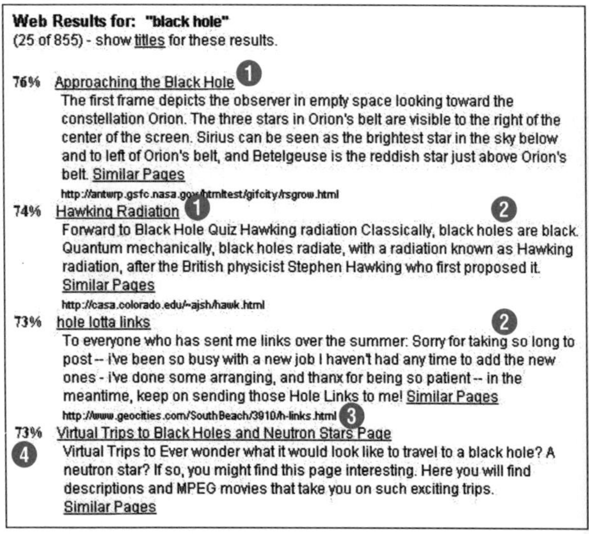

Web Results for: "black hole"
(25 of 855) - show titles for these results.

76% Approaching the Black Hole ①
The first frame depicts the observer in empty space looking toward the constellation Orion. The three stars in Orion's belt are visible to the right of the center of the screen. Sirius can be seen as the brightest star in the sky below and to left of Orion's belt, and Betelgeuse is the reddish star just above Orion's belt. Similar Pages
http://antwrp.gsfc.nasa.gov/htmltest/gifcity/rsgrow.html

74% Hawking Radiation ① ②
Forward to Black Hole Quiz Hawking radiation Classically, black holes are black. Quantum mechanically, black holes radiate, with a radiation known as Hawking radiation, after the British physicist Stephen Hawking who first proposed it. Similar Pages
http://casa.colorado.edu/~ajsh/hawk.html

73% hole lotta links ②
To everyone who has sent me links over the summer: Sorry for taking so long to post -- i've been so busy with a new job I haven't had any time to add the new ones - i've done some arranging, and thanx for being so patient -- in the meantime, keep on sending those Hole Links to me! Similar Pages
http://www.geocities.com/SouthBeach/3910/h-links.html ③

73% ④ Virtual Trips to Black Holes and Neutron Stars Page
Virtual Trips to Ever wonder what it would look like to travel to a black hole? A neutron star? If so, you might find this page interesting. Here you will find descriptions and MPEG movies that take you on such exciting trips. Similar Pages

① Title of the source
② Summary information
③ URL, or Internet address
④ Percentage of reliability

FIGURE 2.6 To decide which sources to pursue, scan the information on the search results page carefully. (*Source*: WebCrawler, http://www.webcrawler.com)

of creation or last modification, the language in which
the file is written, and sometimes a link to automatically
translate the text to or from English if necessary (see
Figure 2.7).

The URL for the first item in Figure 2.7, http://www
.ncsa.uiuc.edu/Cyberia/NumRel/BlackHoles.html, indicates that this source is published on the server for an
educational   institution   (http://www.ncsa.uiuc.**edu**).
However, it is impossible to determine from the directory information (**/Cyberia/NumRel/**) whether this site
is sponsored by the university or if it is a student project
(see Section 1.3). The summary information explains
what might be available at the site, helping you to determine its relevance.

The second item in Figure 6.2 appears to be the FAQ
(or frequently asked questions) posting for an Internet
newsgroup named *sci.physics* hosted at http://skyron
.harvard.edu, but, again, there is no way to determine

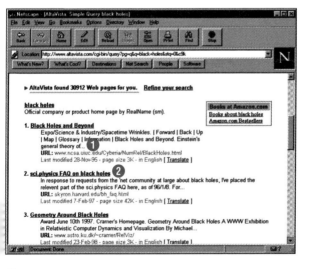

① This source is published on a university site, but it is impossible
to determine the author's authority from the directory information.

② Visiting this Internet newsgroup's FAQ file is the only way to
determine its usefulness or reliability.

FIGURE 2.7 Evaluating Internet publication information.
(*Source: AltaVista* search engine, http://www.altavista.com)

from the URL how reliable the information might be. Of course, the only way to know how important a site may be to your research is to visit it: simply point your cursor to the hypertext link for the item and click on it. Sometimes these sites lead to more indexes and more links until, eventually, you find the information you want. Sometimes you need to return to the search engine and start again.

It won't take long for you to discover that surfing the Web for information can be time-consuming and frustrating. The results of searches can be overwhelming, and, worse, many "hits" will not prove useful or relevant; in addition, searches often return multiple listings of the same site. In such cases, you may need to repeat your search, using different terms or even different engines or directories. Be patient, however. You'll quickly learn the ins and outs of Web searching.

2.3.2   **Email.**   Electronic mail (or email), listservs, and Internet newsgroups can also be valuable sources of information for a research project, offering sites from which to ask questions or to find out about other sources. Some asynchronous forums, such as email lists and newsgroups, are informal or classroom discussion lists. Others, such as clari.net, are fee-for-subscription services that offer up-to-the-hour news reporting. Newsgroups themselves come in all sizes and flavors, from raunchy "alt.whatever" free-for-alls to moderated groups offering expert information on a wide variety of topics. Many listservs and newsgroups can be scanned using various search engines, and they may archive (that is, store) their past messages.

a   **Email etiquette.**   Most newsgroups and listservs are topic-centered forums, attracting readers with common interests. The difference is that newsgroups are usually open public forums for discussion while listservs may require some sort of subscription process. Some listservs limit their membership or are moderated. (In a moderated list, messages must be approved before being forwarded to the list members.).

How to Connect to Email

SHELL ACCOUNT
Shell accounts usually allow you to compose and read email offline by using your communications software to upload and download mail files. However, shell accounts may also offer online editors. Commands vary, but common UNIX shell email programs can be accessed by typing one of the following commands.

> pine
> elm
> mail

Check with your systems administrator for more information.

PPP ACCOUNT
Many PPP accounts also allow users to use online editors and mail programs. However, you may also use programs installed on your own computer, such as *Netscape Mail, Eudora, Outlook Express* or other point-and-click mail editors to automatically download, read, and compose messages. Graphical User Interface (or GUI) editors allow for the inclusion of graphics, fonts, colors, and links in email; however, unless your reader is using a similar email client program, formatting may not be visible.

Most listservs welcome new members, but before subscribing to a list, check out its FAQ posting if there is one, and then "lurk" for a while, getting a sense of the list's level of conversation and its particular etiquette. Although some groups may discourage students or researchers from asking questions, most listerv members are happy to share their information with students whose questions show thought, knowledge, and advance preparation.

The posting shown in the following box is an email message from a high school student who needed information for a paper on Ernest Hemingway. The listserv to which he posted is made up primarily of graduate students and scholars interested in Ernest Hemingway, but it is open to anyone with an interest in the novelist. Note that the writer begins with an honest acknowledgment that he is a high school student seeking information for an academic assignment. He tells his readers how much he knows about the topic, and, since this is a group of people with an interest in Hemingway, he lets the readers know that he has also enjoyed the readings. He then asks specific questions about the stories,

Date: Wed, 1 May 1997 17:32:22 -0500
From: Steve Brown <sbrown@aol.com>
Reply to: A Discussion of Ernest Hemingway and his works <ERNEST@CFRVM.CFR.USF.EDU>
To: Multiple recipients of list ERNEST<ERNEST@CFRVM.CFR.USF.EDU>
Subject: Green Hills

    I am a high school student who has to do a report on Hemingway, and I was supposed to read _The Old Man and the Sea_ and two other short stories. But I have enjoyed Hemingway's work so I have read about 5 short stories, including the assigned work and _The Green Hills of Africa_. I finished The Green Hills today and am left with many questions that need to be answered.
    In the foreword he states that all stories are true and that the book is completely nonfiction. This is hard for me to understand because of the vivid imagery of many of the animals and how the whole story seems to go the way that much of the life of Hemingway went (the long drought before _The Old Man and the Sea_ and always having someone (Karl) just a little bit luckier than him). Another question: when did he write this book in relationship to when he took this trip? If anyone has any other responses to this book I would be more than happy to hear them also. I have gotten a lot out of the different opinions stated by some of the people in this group. Thanks a lot.

demonstrating that he has done some background work. He does *not* ask the list to do his work for him; instead, he is looking for answers to specific questions. His posting shows respect for the group, and he doesn't waste anyone else's time.

Similar attention to the following guidelines—usually called netiquette, or Internet etiquette—can help make electronic discussions more courteous and productive.

- Read the FAQ (frequently asked questions) posting for the list or newsgroup, if there is one, to get a sense of the conversation and any limitations.

- Avoid the use of all-capital letters. "All caps" is usually considered the electronic equivalent of shouting.

- Do not send advertisements, chain letters, or personal messages to the entire list.

- Postings should be relevant to the topic of the list; for most lists, keep postings as brief as possible.

- When replying to previous messages, quote only those portions of the message to which you are referring.

- It is usually a good idea (and often stipulated in the FAQ) to acquire permission before quoting from or re-posting messages from the list. Do not post copyrighted material from other sources to the list without permission from the copyright owner.

- Include a brief *subject line* that describes the topic of your message. If your message is part of an ongoing thread (that is, a discussion of a particular topic), use the same subject line as the message(s) to which you are replying.

- Keep signature files, if used, brief—usually no more than four lines. (*Signature files* allow writers to attach information about themselves to the end of each email message.)

- Avoid flaming. (A *flame* is a message that attacks another member of the list or his or her beliefs and ideas.) Keep discussions and arguments on topic and courteous.

- Avoid "me, too" messages. Do not reply to the list simply to express agreement; your posting should have something to contribute to the conversation.

- Use acronyms and "emoticons" (smiley faces and other symbols) sparingly. Make sure the members of the list are familiar with those you choose to use, and remember that humor and sarcasm may be hard to express in text-only formats like email.

For more information on netiquette, see *The Net: User Guidelines and Netiquette* by Arlene H. Rinaldi at http://www.fau.edu/rinaldi/netiquette.html.

b Finding information in listservs and newsgroups. To locate particular listservs and newsgroups, you can use a search engine such as *Tile.Net* (http://tile.net) or *Liszt* (http://www.liszt.com). These engines offer searchable indexes of lists and provide information for subscribing to them. Many Internet search engines also search the archives posted by some newsgroups and listservs. Figure 2.8 shows the results of a search of Usenet newsgroups with *Deja.com*. The list-

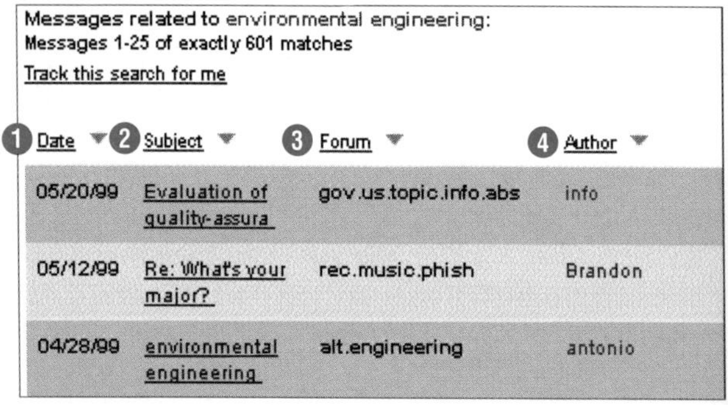

The search results include:
1. The date of the posting
2. The subject line
3. The address of the newsgroup
4. The author's name

FIGURE 2.8 **Search topics in newsgroups. (Source: Deja.com, http://www.deja.com)**

ing of results includes the date of each posting, the subject line of the posting, and the address of the newsgroup. You can preview the messages in your browser or retrieve them from your local server.

Some listservs and newsgroups also archive messages; that is, their messages are stored for later retrieval. Instructions for retrieving archived messages are usually found in the FAQ for the list. Archives stored on the WWW may include searchable indexes and may be readable using a browser. Other archives use specific commands and can be retrieved by sending an email message to the list server.

To decide whether a posting relates to your topic, check its subject line. Similarly, the date of the posting can give you some idea of its currency, and the type of newsgroup can clue you in to the type of information you will find. A list of some of the more common newsgroup identifiers is provided in the following box.

Identifying Newsgroups

alt.	A catchall for "alternative" newsgroups covering almost any topic area
comp.	Discussions centered around various computer-related topics
misc.	Miscellaneous topics that don't fit easily into other categories
news.	Local, national, or world events and occurrences
rec.	Discussions of recreational pastimes and related interests
sci.	Topics centered around areas of interest to the sciences
soc.	Sociological issues and cultural discussions
talk.	Usually informal discussion groups that are more social in nature

---

For example, the newsgroup *sci.physics.electromag* offers discussions of electromagnetic theory. Newsgroup identifiers may also include a prefix designating a specific locale; for instance, *uiuc.misc.environment* is a newsgroup hosted by the University of Illinois at Urbana-Champaign that discusses environment-related issues.

The only way to evaluate the usefulness of a given posting is to read it. In evaluating a group, scan a reasonable selection of its messages to learn whether its conversation might benefit your research. And, since many listservs and newsgroups are public forums to which anyone can send messages, be prepared to check other, more authoritative sources to verify any information you take from such postings. However, do recognize that listserv and newsgroup discussions can help you learn where to find reliable information, in print or online. And when you are researching a controversial topic, these groups may give you a realistic feel for the territory of the debate—what the extreme positions are, who's in the middle, what issues are in contention.

2.3.3   File transfer protocol (FTP).   FTP stands for file transfer protocol, but the same abbreviation is used to name the sites and many of the programs that use the protocol. You use an FTP program to log on to an FTP site (the computer host) so you can download files using FTP (the protocol). Computer users can use FTP to upload and download text files; graphics, audio, and video files; software; and much more from sites around the world. Although you can use the FTP protocol in a command-line interface, most WWW browsers are now configured to access these sites and download any information you find; or you can use an FTP client program (see Figure 2.10, p. 62) to upload and download files. Some FTP sites require that users have an account on the system in order to access the files contained there; however, many also offer anonymous FTP (users log on as "anonymous" and type their email address as a password).

One drawback of FTP sites is that the information may not be readable until after you retrieve and download the files—which can be a time-consuming process. One key is to understand online terminology so that at least you will ensure that the file you download will be readable or usable when you're done. Many computer systems automatically recognize the programs associated with various file extensions. However, you may need to

How to Connect to an FTP Site

SHELL ACCOUNT

Shell accounts usually allow you to access FTP sites by typing one of the following commands.

> ftp
> ncftp

For sites that allow anonymous FTP, use the log-in ID "anonymous" and enter your complete email address as your password. Commands are entered using a command-line interface. Once connected, type "help" for a listing of commands. Check with your systems administrator for more information.

PPP ACCOUNT

Many PPP accounts also allow for the use of FTP client programs to move information between locations. You can use FTP clients to move files from your personal computer to your Internet server account or from other FTP servers. To connect to sites that allow anonymous FTP, use the log-in ID "anonymous" and your complete email address as your password.

tell the system which application to associate with various types of files, if prompted. Browsers such as Netscape *Navigator* can also be configured to open the necessary applications (or plug-ins) if necessary. Some common file extensions are listed in the box on the next page.

Some formats are readable by more than one application; other formats require specific software. Sometimes information is compressed to speed upload or download time and may require specific applications to uncompress or view files, or you may be able to find information to help you by using an Internet search engine and searching for the file extension.

Most search engines search FTP sites as well as WWW sites, and files can often be retrieved using a Web browser and the ftp://address format (for example, ftp://ftp.whatever.com). Figure 2.9 shows a typical FTP directory accessed using an Internet Web browser.

FTP sites can also be searched using the FTP search protocol *Archie,* which gathers information from

Common File Extensions

TEXT FORMATS

.doc	*Word* or *WordPerfect*
.latex	LaTeX file
.pdf	portable document format
.ps	PostScript file
.rtf	Rich Text format
.tex	TeX file
.txt, .text	ASCII or *Simple Text*
.wpd	*WordPerfect*

AUDIO, VIDEO, AND GRAPHICS FILES

.au	audio file
.avi	movie file
.bmp	Windows Bitmap graphics format
.gif	graphics files
.jpg, .jpeg	graphics files
.mov, .qt	Apple *QuickTime* movie
.mpg, .mpeg	audio and video formats
.ra, .ram	RealAudio formats
.tif, .tiff	graphics files
.wav, .wave	audio file

PRESENTATION FORMATS

.ppt	*PowerPoint* presentation
.shw	Corel presentation

APPLICATION FORMATS

.bat	batch file
.exe	executable file
.js	Java script
.pl	Perl script

COMPRESSION FORMATS

.arj	file archiving
.gz, .gzip	compression format
.hqx	Macintosh BinHex compression
.lha	file compression format
.zip	PkZip compression

MULTIMEDIA FORMATS

.htm, .html	HyperText Markup Language
.vrml	Virtual Reality Markup Language

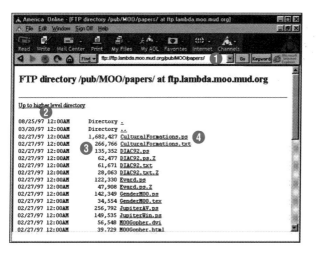

FTP directory /pub/MOO/papers/ at ftp.lambda.moo.mud.org

Up to higher level directory

08/25/97 12:00AM	Directory	.
03/20/97 12:00AM	Directory	..
02/27/97 12:00AM	1,682,427	CulturalFormations.ps
02/27/97 12:00AM	266,766	CulturalFormations.txt
02/27/97 12:00AM	135,352	DIAC92.ps
02/27/97 12:00AM	62,477	DIAC92.ps.Z
02/27/97 12:00AM	61,671	DIAC92.txt
02/27/97 12:00AM	28,063	DIAC92.txt.Z
02/27/97 12:00AM	122,330	Evard.ps
02/27/97 12:00AM	47,908	Evard.ps.Z
02/27/97 12:00AM	142,349	GenderMOO.ps
02/27/97 12:00AM	34,554	GenderMOO.tex
02/27/97 12:00AM	256,792	JupiterAV.ps
02/27/97 12:00AM	149,535	JupiterWin.ps
02/27/97 12:00AM	56,548	MOOGopher.dvi
02/27/97 12:00AM	39,729	MOOGopher.html

1 Use the address form ftp://whatever to access FTP sites using a browser.

FTP directories may include various information:

2 Electronic publication date

3 File size

4 File name and extension

FIGURE 2.9 **An FTP directory accessed using a Web browser.** (*Source: Lambda* MOO's FTP server at ftp://ftp.lambda.moo.mud.org/pub/MOO/papers/)

anonymous FTP sites and indexes them for search and retrieval (see http://opim.wharton.upenn.edu/~serdar93/ internet/archie.html). Files may be available in a choice of formats, designated by the file extension, sozme of which are readable online and some of which must be downloaded and opened in a separate application. The FTP directory also lists the date of creation or last modification and the size of the file.

You can also search through FTP sites by moving through the directories using your browser or an FTP client program such as the one shown in Figure 2.10. Unfortunately, you may not be able to read many of these files until after you download them. Pay careful attention, therefore, to date, title, author, and publication information, if available, to help you ascertain whether

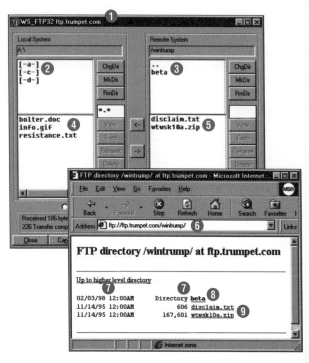

1. The address of the remote host
2. Your local drives
3. Subdirectories on the remote host
4. Local files
5. Files on the remote host
6. Address of the remote host
7. Information about directories and files
8. Directories on the remote host
9. Files on the remote host

FIGURE 2.10 Access FTP sites using an FTP client or your Internet browser.

the sources might be useful for your project. If a description of the file or text is available online, read it carefully to ensure that the time you spend downloading the file won't be wasted.

In Figure 2.10, the FTP client program shows the local directory on the left-hand side (in this case, the a:\ drive on a personal computer) and the remote host, an

FTP site at ftp.trumpet.com, on the right-hand side. The top portion of each side shows the drives and directories (wintrump is the directory on the remote host, and beta is a subdirectory of wintrump). The bottom portion of each side shows the files contained in the directory. To move files from one location to another using the client program, simply highlight the file and click on the arrow in the direction you wish to move the file. The three-letter file extension is the only clue you have to the types of files: for example, disclaim.txt is a text file, and wtwsk10a.zip is a compressed file that will require an "unzip" utility to open. There is no way to know, however, what is contained in the compressed file. The text file may give more information, but it is necessary to download this file in order to read it. By accessing the site using a Web browser and the URL ftp://ftp.trumpet.com/wintrump/, you can get more information, including the size of each file and the date of its creation. You can also read the text file on the Web, obtaining more information that may help you to determine whether the file will be useful before you download it. You can download compressed files in your browser by clicking on the hypertext link (in this case, the file name).

2.3.4   Telnet applications.   Telnet is an application that allows you to log on to a remote computer host and access its files and programs. Most telnet sites require you to have an account on their server, with a log-in name and password. Once connected, you can work on that computer (the host) just as if you had accessed it directly. You may be able to use telnet protocols to log on to your school computer from home, and many libraries allow telnet access to their catalogs. If your browser is configured with a telnet client, you can access these sites using the telnet://address format (for example, telnet://damoo.csun.edu:7777). There are various client programs often available for free downloading on the Internet, to help you access these sites.

In addition to connecting to your server or to the library, telnet protocols allow you to connect to synchronous communication sites on the Internet where multi-

How to Connect to Telnet

SHELL ACCOUNT

UNIX shell accounts usually allow for access to telnet sites by typing

> telnet ⟨address⟩ ⟨port#⟩ (for example, telnet damoo.csun.edu 7777)

For VAX systems, type

> telnet ⟨address/port=port#⟩ (for example, telnet damoo.csun.edu/port=7777)

Check with your systems administrator for the commands to use on your system.

PPP ACCOUNT

Many PPP accounts allow the use of telnet client programs to connect to remote hosts. Client programs reside on your personal computer. Many different telnet clients are available for free download on the Internet, or your Internet service provider may provide directions for installing telnet clients configured to work with their system (for example, if you are connected through America Online you may need to install and use a telnet client specifically configured for AOL; you can find information under "Keyword: telnet" online).

To connect to MOOs and MUDs, various client programs are available in addition to telnet clients, many of them free. For more information on finding and downloading client software, see "Client Software for MUDs and/or MOOs" at http://ebbs.english.vt.edu/mudmoo.clients.html.

You can also connect to telnet sites using your Web browser (provided it is configured to recognize the telnet client program) by typing "telnet://address:port" (for example, telnet://damoo.csun.edu:7777).

ple users can log on and communicate with each other in real time. That is, commands sent by users appear on each other's screens almost immediately. Many of these sites host scholarly conferences and classes; some, such as the *Internet Public Library* MOO and a number of on-line writing labs, offer real-time help with research or writing; and some house various files and objects that may be of use in your research. Synchronous communication sites such as Internet Relay Chat (IRC) or MOOs also offer sites for real-time discussion and interviews with experts.

How to access discussions in synchronous communication sites depends on the type of connection you use. Some sites explicitly request that you ask permission from participants before using any materials (see the box below). Whether you are explicitly asked or not, however, the ethics of research dictate that you obtain permission from all participants before logging any conversations. You should also make sure the participants agree to the use you will make of these discussions in your writing. If you are posting your work to the World Wide Web or publishing it in some other form, you may also want to allow your participants the chance to see not only the portion of the conversation that will be included but also the context in which it will be used.

NOTICE FOR JOURNALISTS AND RESEARCHERS: The citizens of LambdaMOO request that you ask for permission from all direct participants before quoting any material collected here.

From *LambdaMOO* (telnet://lambda.moo.mud.org:8888)

Some real-time conferences make logs available via the World Wide Web. Since these logs are published, you may include portions of them in your work, with proper citation, of course. Pay attention, however, to any disclaimers or information for researchers on these sites as well (for example, the logs of a real-time weekly discussion of issues involved in computers and writing are available on the WWW at http://bsuvc.bsu.edu/ ~00gjsiering/netoric/netoric.html, but with the provision that writers request permission from individual participants before using information contained in them).

Real-time discussions can, of course, support research in many ways. Discussing your ideas in these forums may help you narrow your topic or guide you to sources of information you haven't considered. Online, you may be able to meet and interview experts in the field or conduct ethnographic and field studies, if appropriate. However, using information from these sites may also require additional precautions. Many of these sites allow participants to use aliases or to take on the role of fictitious characters; thus, it may be difficult to determine the authority, if any, of participants. Moreover, files and characters may be temporary or may change without notice. Hence, you should verify any information you obtain from these sites by checking other, more traditional sources as well. You'll have to exercise your best critical skills. (See 1.3 on evaluating sources.)

MOOS AND MUDS. MOO is an acronym for "MUD, Object-Oriented," and MUD stands for "Multi-User Dimension" or "Dungeon," reflecting its origin as a form of the Dungeons and Dragons game developed for multiple players on the Internet. Most MUDs still retain this game-like flavor, with participants attaining higher levels, often by "shooting" and "killing" other players. MOOs, however, have developed into more social spaces, lending themselves readily to use in the classroom and as spaces for conferences and meetings. Other sites include MUCKs, MUSHes, MUSEs, and a proliferation of other related formats.

In addition to providing forums for real-time discussion, MOOs may publish various texts and files. Most MOOs offer mailing lists, similar to newsgroup forums. Even the object descriptions, notes, programming scripts, and other information available in these sites may provide a researcher with useful information. Many MOOs are also "Webbed," meaning that all objects (including players) automatically generate WWW pages on the host site, and characters may edit these WWW pages to suit their needs and desires. Some, such as the *Internet Public Library* MOO, offer real-time help to researchers, and some online writing labs (OWLs) use MOOs to offer real-time help with writing concerns as well. Learning to navigate and communicate in MOOs in order to find information may, however, be a time-consuming process. Make sure you consider the time you have for your project when you decide where to search for information.

The simplest way to connect to a MOO, though perhaps not the easiest to follow, is by using telnet. For example, in a UNIX environment, at your prompt type "telnet damoo.csun.edu 7777" to get access. Most veteran MOOers began with telnet. The only real problem with telnet is that words from other participants may suddenly appear on your screen, interrupting the words you are typing. The MOO ignores the interruptions; you can simply continue typing until you're done and then depress the enter key. However, these interruptions can be confusing, especially when you are first learning to work in a MOO environment.

Client programs can help make MOO life much easier. A client called *Tiny Fugue* can be downloaded from http://tf.tcp.com/~hawkeye/tf/ and installed in your UNIX directory. *Tiny Fugue* provides a separate typing area at the bottom of your screen, and it has built-in help of its own. It also allows you to edit MOO messages, import and export files, and save addresses and log-in names, and there are many more features. To connect to a MOO using *Tiny Fugue*, try typing "tf" at your host prompt. Check with your service provider or systems administrator for more information.

There are also many client programs that offer easy point-and-click interfaces. Most of these are free and can be downloaded from the WWW or from various FTP sites. Usually, they are installed on your computer's hard drive and require a PPP (or point-to-point protocol) connection to use. For a list of some popular client programs available for different *platforms*, see Talon Gaming Network's "Client Index" at http://www.talon .org/TGN/ClientSoftware/.

Most MOOs grow up around a central theme. For example, the theme of *PMC MOO* is postmodern culture, and *BioMOO* is a virtual meeting place for biologists. There are foreign-language MOOs as well, such as *MOOsaico* in Portugal and the French-speaking *SchoolNet MOO* in Canada. Others, such as *Diversity University MOO* and *DaMOO*, offer spaces for classroom meetings and objects designed specifically for use in the classroom. Some MOO addresses are listed in the box below.

MOOs allow for much more than conversation, of course, but their steep learning curve may require an investment in time beyond that allotted for your research

Selected List of MOO Addresses

MOO NAME	TELNET ADDRESS
AtheMOO	moo.hawaii.edu: 9999
AussieMOO	farrer.riv.csu.edu.au 7777
Bay MOO	baymoo.sfsu.edu 8888
BioMOO	bioinformatics.weizmann.ac.il 8888
BushMOO	bushnet.qld.edu.au 7777
Connections	connections.moo.mud.org 3333
DaMOO	damoo.csun.edu 7777
DaedalusMOO	moo.daedalus.com 7777
Diversity University	moo.du.org 8888
Enviro-MOO	avatar.phys-plant.utoledo.edu 5555
EON MOO	mcmuse.mc.maricopa.edu 8888
GNA-Lab MOO	gnalab.uva.nl 7777
Internet Public Library	ipl.sils.umich.edu 8888
LambdaMOO	lambda.moo.mud.org 8888
LinguaMOO	lingua.utdallas.edu 8888
MediaMOO	purple-crayon.media.mit.edu 8888
MOOsaico	moo.di.uminho.pt 7777
Mundo Hispano	europa.syr.edu 8888
PMC MOO	hero.village.virginia.edu 7777
Sensemedia MOO	sprawl.sensemedia.net 7777
SchoolNet MOO (English)	schoolnet.ingenia.com 7777
SchoolNet MOO (French)	moo.rescol.ca 7777
TecfaMOO	tecfamoo.unige.ch 7777
Virtual Online University	athena.edu 8888

project. However, with just a few simple commands, as shown in the table on page 70, you can begin your exploration, and most veteran MOOers—if asked nicely—are friendly and willing to help newbies (newcomers to the MOO) find their way around.

WWW ADDRESS

http://silo.riv.csu.edu.au/AussieMOO.html

http://bioinfo.weizmann.ac.il:8888/

http://www.ucet.ufl.edu/~tari/connections/
   connections-home.html
http://damoo.csun.edu: 8888

http://moo.du.org:8000/
http://www.phys-plant.utoledo.edu:5656/

http://www.ipl.org/moo/

http://lingua.utdallas.edu:7000/

http://sensemedia.net/sprawl
http://moo.schoolnet.ca:7780/eng/

http://moo.rescol.ca:7780/fr/

http://tecfa.unige.ch/tecfamoo.html
http://www.athena.edu/

Some Helpful MOO Command

TYPE THIS ...

say Hi. *or* "Hi.

:wiggles her toes.

page Kiwi Are you here?

@who

look

look Kiwi

@go #<room #>
(for example, @go #11)

@join <character>
(for example, @join Kiwi)

@describe <whatever> as <whatever>
(for example,@describe Kiwi as You see
a teacher standing before you, her hair
in a bun and carrying a large ruler.

@gender <whatever>
(for example, @gender female)

help

@quit

IRC AND CHAT ROOMS Probably one of the most popular programs for real-time synchronous communication is Internet Relay Chat, or IRC. Like MOOs and
MUDs, IRC provides forums or *channels* for real-time
discussion centered around various topics. Chats may

YOU WILL SEE ...	OTHERS IN THE ROOM SEE ...
You say, "Hi."	Guest says, "Hi."
Guest wiggles her toes.	Guest wiggles her toes.
Your message has been sent to Kiwi.	*Others in the room don't see anything but Kiwi sees:* Guest is looking for you in Pub. She pages, "Are you there?"
A listing of everyone who is currently connected to the MOO.	
A description of the room you are in.	
A description of the character named Kiwi.	
Teleports you to the room with that object number (#11 is usually the main room of a MOO).	
Teleports you to whatever room Kiwi is in.	
If you type look me *you will see your description.*	
Sets your character's gender; commands automatically substitute the correct pronouns.	
A list of topics on which help is available.	
Takes you out of the virtual world.	

attract visitors from around the world. Conversations in a chat room can be useful to the researcher, providing ideas to help refine a topic or offering help with locating additional sources of information. These sites also support real-time interviews, sometimes including meetings with celebrities or experts on various topics. IRC conversations can be logged, but you will need to ask for permission before doing so. Like MOOs and MUDs, participants in IRCs may use aliases, so determining the authority of a source may be difficult. You may need to verify information with other, more traditional sources to ensure the validity of information you present in your own work.

IRC hosts are usually accessed by using one of a variety of client programs available for downloading on the Internet. A client may already be installed on your host server (try typing "irc" in your shell account). Many other popular Web-based chat programs and service providers such as America Online offer chat programs for use by subscribers, including AOL's popular *Homework Help Room*. For more information on Internet chat programs, see Yahoo's page at http://www.yahoo.com/ Computers_and_Internet/Internet/Chat/ or check with your local service provider.

2.3.5 **Gopher.** On the Internet, documents, files, and directories are structured like the directory tree you may already be familiar with in the Windows *File Manager* or *Explorer* programs. Gopher, one of the earliest protocols for locating online information, uses a menu-driven system to find and retrieve documents and files. Although Gopher is being replaced on many sites by hypertext protocols, many Gopher sites still offer valuable information that may not be easily searchable via the Web. Gopherspace can be searched using its own search protocols, *Veronica* and *Jughead*. *Veronica* searches all the gopher servers in the world using keywords. *Jughead* searches titles in gopherspace for keywords, much like *Veronica*, but allows you to limit your search to specific gopher servers. You can also use WWW search engines to access and search for much of the information in gopherspace. For more information on searching gopherspace, see http://www.terena.nl/ libr/gnrt/explore/gopher.html.

Figure 2.11 shows a typical Gopher directory accessed using a graphical browser (Netscape *Navigator*)

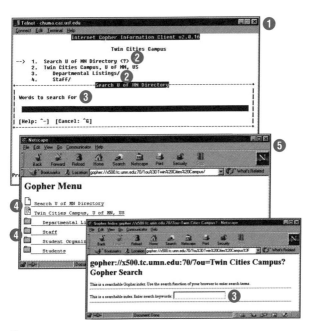

1. Gopher directories can be accessed using a shell account and the Gopher protocol.
2. Search directories are designated by a question mark; subdirectories are indicated by the forward slash mark (/).
3. Use keyword searching to locate files.
4. Icons indicate whether the link is a text file or a directory.
5. Gopher directories can also be accessed using a browser.

FIGURE 2.11 Gopher sites can be accessed and searched using a shell account and Gopher protocols or a Web browser.

and using the Gopher protocol in a shell account. In the graphical browser, the type of link is designated by the appropriate icon. A piece of paper with writing on it indicates a text file, file folders indicate directories (which contain more lists of information), and so on. In the text browser, text documents are the default, links ending with the forward slash mark / indicate directories, and other types of files (such as graphics or movies) are indicated by enclosing the file type in angle brackets ⟨ ⟩ after the link name.

How to Connect to Gopher Sites

SHELL ACCOUNT

Shell accounts usually allow you to access Gopher sites by typing "gopher" followed by a space and the address of the Gopher server. You may also be able to access Gopher sites through *Lynx* (a text-only WWW browser often available in shell accounts) by using the gopher:// address.wherever.edu form. You can get information on Gopher commands by typing "?" when you are connected to a Gopher server.

PPP ACCOUNT

Most PPP accounts allow you to connect to Gopher sites using the gopher://address.wherever.edu form in your WWW browser. You can then move through directories by pointing to the desired directory. Gopher clients can be downloaded and installed on your computer to allow for easy graphical point-and-click interfaces, such as *WinGopher* (for Windows platforms) or *The Guide* (available for both Windows and Macintosh platforms). For more information, see gopher://gopher.tc.umn.edu and follow the directories "Information About Gopher" and "Gopher Software Distribution."

Many Gopher files can be read online in your Gopher client. Some files, however, come in formats that must be downloaded and opened in another application on your computer. (See Section 1.3.1 for more information on identifying file extensions and the applications with which they are associated.) If you are accessing the files using a shell account, you may need to save the file to your host directory and then use your communications software package to download it to your computer. Graphical user interface or GUI browsers, however, can usually save the files directly to your hard drive or disk. Since gopher addresses are often long and unwieldy, you may choose to cite either the direct URL or the Gopher address for a file or to list the address for a host site followed by the directories used to access the specific file (see Part 4 for more on citing Gopher files).

2 . 4

Other Online Sources

In addition to the Internet and library databases, online information services and bulletin board services (BBSs) offer an array of files, programs, chat room discussions, newsgroups, forums, channels, reference sources, and other information. Many BBSs are local and are accessed similarly to the Internet: you dial a local number and connect, usually as a visitor until you request an account. Many BBSs are free and may offer Internet access of varying amounts, usually access to email and **Bitnet** or Usenet newsgroups. Some of the larger commercial online services, such as America Online and Prodigy, also offer customers access to WWW browsers and space on their servers to publish home pages. It is important, however, to differentiate between Internet sources and BBS sources, since many information services and BBSs can be accessed only by fee-paying subscribers. For instance, America Online offers subscribers access to articles in *Consumer Reports* using a searchable index; subscribers to other online services may not be able to access this information without paying an additional fee.

2.4.1 **BBSs and local forums.** BBS newsgroups and forums usually are similar to Internet newsgroups and listservs in that they are centered around areas of interest. For instance, the BBS for Stetson Law University in St. Petersburg, Florida, has forums for women and gender issues, AIDS activism, information about courses and policies of the university, and many other topics of interest to its subscribers. Microsoft Network (MSN) offers forums covering a range of topics from the adult students forum, with discussions centered on lifelong learning, to the writing forum, a meeting place for authors and poets. Postings are similar to email messages, usually with a subject line and often with a place to quote the message to which you are responding. The biggest difference between Internet newsgroups and BBS forums is that Internet newsgroups may attract people from all over the word; BBS forums are limited to subscribers only. The larger commercial services, of course, number their subscribers in the millions, and even many local BBSs may include access to Internet newsgroups in their lists.

2.4.2 **Subscriber encyclopedias and other reference sources.** Some network services, especially the larger commercial ones, offer online reference sources to their subscribers. For instance, America Online offers access to several different dictionaries and encyclopedias, including the *Merriam-Webster Dictionary, Compton's Encyclopedia, The Concise Columbia Encyclopedia,* and *Grolier's Multimedia Encyclopedia,* all with searchable indexes, plus other online reference sources. Also available are links to WWW sources such as *Bartlett's Familiar Quotations* and the *Internet Public Library.* Magazines, newspapers, and news services are also offered at no additional fee to subscribers; actual news videos can even be downloaded and viewed on your computer. In addition to providing access to published reference sources, many larger services also offer online courses and message centers where you can ask experts for help on various topics. For example, America Online offers tutoring rooms where you can get help from teachers in real time. Again, some of this information is available only to subscribers, so in documenting such a resource, it is important to note the name of the online service if applicable. (See Part 4 for more on documentation.)

2.4.3 **Chat rooms and other local sites.** Many BBSs and online services also offer synchronous communication sites called chat rooms similar to IRC (Internet Relay Chat). Like IRC, these rooms are grouped around topics of interest to members. Subscribers can get help with homework, ask questions of experts, meet celebrities online, get technical support, or just chat with online friends. MSN chat rooms cover topics ranging from Alcoholics Anonymous to women's health issues; AOL offers chats covering a wide range of topics in addition to specially scheduled chat sessions with celebrities or experts from a variety of fields. Some services also offer various forms of MUDs for subscribers. Again, it is important to differentiate between Internet sources and subscriber sources, although it may not always be easy to tell the difference.

2.4.4   Software and video games.   Software and video games can sometimes be sources of information, too. Video games, for example, can be used as examples of popular culture or as examples of how violence is portrayed in our society. Software programs usually have extensive online help files; for example, a paper on how writing is changing in the electronic age might cite *WordPerfect*'s "Grammatik," which lists rules for punctuation, sentence structure, and other elements of writing. Microsoft's popular *PowerPoint* program includes such useful information as "The 'Four P's' for Better Presenting" by Dale Carnegie Training, which can help you create better presentations and also provide information for a paper or project. Even bookkeeping software may explain accounting principles, small-business management, or tax information.

Keeping Track

Whether you are conducting research on the WWW, using an online information service, or searching an online library catalog, you need to keep track of what you find. Careful management of information will keep you from duplicating effort in your research and will ensure that you have adequate information to cite your sources accurately. Perhaps the simplest way to keep track of the information you find is to keep a set of 3-by-5-inch bibliography cards, listing one source on each card. Note cards will prove invaluable when you assemble the Works Cited or References pages required in most standard academic projects. Each bibliography card should contain all the information you would need to find a source again later, plus the date of publication (if known) along with the date of access for Internet sources, as well as the author's name and the title of the work. (For more on the elements of electronic citations, see Part 4.) A typical bibliography card looks like this.

CNN Interactive. "Shuttle Atlantis
    Makes Repair Call to Mir."
    17 May 1997.
    http://www.cnn.com/TECH/9705/
    16/shuttle/index.html (19 May 1997).

Be sure to include any other information necessary to access the source, such as a directory path, links, or file or accession numbers if appropriate. For library sources, include the call number in the upper left-hand corner.

2.5.1   Cut and paste.   Instead of preparing traditional bibliography cards, you may wish to cut and paste URLs and other important information, such as direct quotations, directly into your word processing or database file. This technique will help to ensure accuracy when copying information. Make sure you note other important information about the source, such as the author's name, the title of the site, the date of publication, and the date of access (see also Part 4), so that you will not duplicate your efforts. Creating an electronic database or word-processing file that lists your sources can make it easy to rearrange sources by fields that you designate, such as the author's name, the date of publication, or keywords you assign. Check the help-file in your software for how-to information. You can easily search these files for keywords or phrases instead of having to shuffle through an entire deck of note cards in order to find a specific reference.

2.5.2 **Download or print out files.**   Sometimes you may wish to download or print out files that you intend to use in your work, especially if online access to these sites is difficult or uncertain. If the source is archived, you should attempt to locate the address or directory path to access the file in the archive. However, if information is posted to an online site for only a limited amount of time, you may instead want to print it or download it and save it on your hard drive or a disk. Make sure, however, to keep an accurate record of where the information came from, including the electronic address or path and the date you accessed the information. Many browsers can automatically include this information on printed copies of Web sites (check the page setup configuration in your browser if this information does not appear). However, when you download files, this information is usually not included; you will need to create a separate file or note card that lists information about each downloaded entry.

Printed copies of online library or database screens can be especially useful. Figure 2.12 shows a typical library catalog entry. The screen can be printed or saved to a computer file. It provides all the information necessary for a bibliography entry, including the author's full name, the title of the book, and the publication information. In addition, the entry notes the location and call number of the work. You can annotate these pages to include notes about the work, either on screen or on printed copies. You may be able to open the page in your word processor or HTML editor, then cut and paste information directly into your final project.

2.5.3 **Use your bookmarks file.**   Most browsers allow you to save addresses of sites you visit, making a bookmarks file to help you find information again as

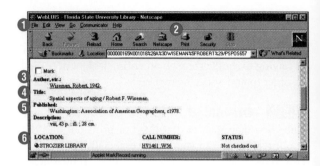

1 Save a Web page as plain text (.txt) or HTML to use in other applications.

2 Print a copy of the file, or copy and paste information into other applications.

The library catalog entry provides:

3 Author

4 Title

5 Publication information

6 Location information

FIGURE 2.12 Save information from the library catalog by downloading or printing the file.

in Figure 2.13. Your browser may call this a "favorites" file. In text-only browsers such as *Lynx*, you can save bookmarks in the "Options" menu or email the information to yourself. Many browsers also allow you to organize your bookmarks into folders. You can also save your bookmarks file to a floppy disk, especially useful if you will be working on different computers or in open-use labs on campus.

2.5.4 Electronic note cards and bibliography programs. Commercial software programs can help you record important information about your sources, including bibliographic information as well as direct quotations or other notes about a source. Software packages such as *Pro-Cite*, *BiblioCite Pro*, *Citation*, and *Q-Notes* are available for various platforms, or you can create your own forms using a database program or a

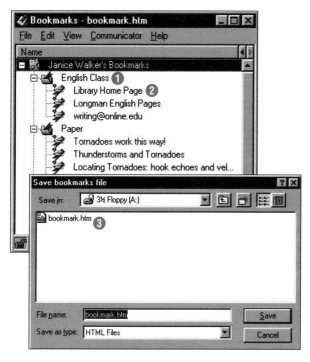

① Create folders to organize information in your bookmarks file.
② Save useful Web sites in your bookmarks file for easy access.
③ Save your bookmarks file to disk for portability.

FIGURE 2.13 Bookmarks files can help you keep track of Web sites.

word processing application. These packages allow you to capture information electronically and keep track of it in order to accurately cite your sources and compile your bibliography. Figure 2.14 shows screens in *Citation7 for Windows* that can automatically generate bibliographical lists or format in-text entries following whatever style you are required to use. Built-in templates for various types of sources help you list the necessary information. Some of these software packages can be configured to work from inside your word processor to help you ensure that your citations are accurate.

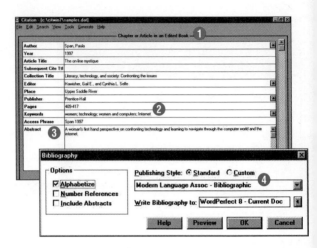

1. Bibliography programs supply templates to ensure that required information is not missed.

2. Include keywords to help you locate information quickly.

3. An abstract, a quotation or paraphrase, or summary information is keyed to the source. Include page numbers when applicable.

4. Programs automatically generate bibliographies and in-text citations.

FIGURE 2.14 Bibliography programs can help ensure the accuracy of your citations. (*Source:* Oberon's *Citation7 for Windows,* http://www.oberon-res.com)

P A R T 3

Designing Your Project

SECTION 3.1
Design Considerations

SECTION 3.2
Designing Print Documents

SECTION 3.3
Designing Electronic Documents

SECTION 3.4
Putting Together a Basic Web Page

What shape should your project take? Depending on your purpose and audience, you might design a traditional classroom paper, a manuscript for publication in a journal, a slide presentation, or, perhaps, an HTML file for uploading to the World Wide Web. Many factors guide such choices, and, of course, an instructor, editor, or supervisor may simply determine the format of a project for you.

This section will help you choose among possible formats, grasp their elements, and learn principles of design for both print and electronic documents. Within the scope of this book, we cannot offer detailed formatting instructions for all available word-processing programs or Web design applications. Nor do we intend to lay down hard-and-fast rules for document design—there aren't many. Instead, we'll suggest guidelines to consider when you prepare a project, along with brief samples of the kind of work you may be expected to produce.

Much advice here is taken from *The Columbia Guide to Online Style* (Columbia UP, 1998), which provides standards for producing three basic types of academic projects.

- Essays written to be printed out, such as for the classroom
- Manuscripts to be submitted to publishers for print publication
- Academic essays to be published electronically in HTML

In addition, we include procedures for producing other types of documents, such as brochures, résumés, and electronic presentations. You may also want to consult the specific stylebook for your discipline, works such as the following:

- *MLA Handbook for Writers of Research Papers*, 5th edition
- *Publication Manual of the American Psychological Association*, 4th edition
- *The Chicago Manual of Style*, 14th edition
- *A Manual for Writers of Term Papers, Theses, and Dissertations*, 6th edition, by Kate L. Turabian

For more information on HTML authoring, consult *A Beginner's Guide to HTML* by the National Center for Supercomputing Applications (NCSA) at http://www.ncsa.uiuc.edu/General/Internet/WWW/HTMLPrimer.html or the *Web Style Guide* by the Yale Center for Advanced Instructional Media (C/AIM) at http://info.med.yale.edu/caim/manual/.

Design Considerations

Once you have determined a focus for your project and gathered the information you want to present, you can determine the best format to use. This section presents some factors to consider to help you determine which format is the best one for your purpose, along with some important design considerations for both print and electronic documents.

3.1.1   **Determining your format.**   To determine a format for your final project, consider factors such as the following.

- Your purpose in preparing the project
- The potential audience(s) for the project
- The time available to complete the project
- Your access to necessary equipment and programs, such as presentation or desktop publishing software, scanners, or graphics programs
- Your technical skill in using that equipment.

a **Purpose.**   Regardless of the framework you choose for your project, you need to make a point. Will your purpose be to persuade? to inform? to entertain? to move to action? The design of your project will have to support such goals. Quite often, your purpose may be obvious: a college project designed generally to present information will likely follow a familiar academic format such as that recommended by the MLA or APA style manual.

But purposes can also be much more narrow and pragmatic. For example, if one purpose of a project is to encourage readers to respond to your work, you'll have to make it easy for them to do so—perhaps by furnishing an email address, a telephone number, or a mailing address. Or if you want readers to pressure their congressional representatives on an issue, your project might include a list of the representatives' names and addresses, as well as a sample letter identifying key points to make. For similar reasons, brochures and mailings might include tear-off response forms, and your résumé would list contact information in addition to outlining your job qualifications. Indeed, the format you choose for your résumé is particularly important because it, too, demonstrates your grasp of effective communication skills.

b **Audience.** The intended audience will, of course, influence the design of your work. For instance, academic audiences (instructors, colleagues in a field, students) likely have expectations that differ substantially from those of business executives or more general readers. Analyze the needs and capabilities of any audience you hope to address.

- What information is your typical reader likely to already have?
- What materials will you have to furnish?
- What tools will your intended audience need in order to gain access to the information you provide?

Then you need to provide cues for navigating your project. In traditional papers, such cues may be as basic as transitional words and phrases or headings and subheadings. Or they may be as complex as graphs, tables, or full appendixes.

For electronic documents, the navigation requirements may be quite different. On a WWW home page, you may need to supply hypertext links or page anchors, as well as instructions for downloading any applications or plug-ins readers will need in order to use your site. You'll also want to offer your information in formats that general audiences can readily access. For Web sites, for example, that may mean avoiding the use of Java scripts or other advanced programming techniques if most readers in your audience can't open them. Keep in mind, too, that readers may want to print copies of WWW documents. When that's the case, be sure that all important elements of your electronic document will survive the translation into print. (For instance, be sure that the URLs for your links will be visible in printed copies.)

Consider, too, the best media to reach your intended audience(s): by mail, by telephone, in person, in print, or via email or the WWW? You may even need to combine or overlap formats to reach your whole audience. For instance, on the World Wide Web, you may want to provide a text-only version of your Web pages (many of which will feature images) to accommodate users without access to graphical browsers such as Netscape *Navigator* or *Internet Explorer* as well as the visually impaired, who may need to access the Web through programs that read texts to them. Similarly, you may decide to offer your materials in simple form by email or in text-only versions on the WWW while also providing them in downloadable formats (such as portable document format, or PDF) that retain your document formatting codes. In any case, always be sure that readers can gain access to the programs necessary to read your documents and files.

c   Time.   The time available to complete your project may determine how you will present it. For instance, you'll have to weigh the benefit of trying a new technology against the time it will take you to learn it. If creating pie charts is a mystery to you, you might want to avoid them in writing a paper due in just a few days. If you have never designed a Web page before, learning advanced HTML authoring techniques may demand more time than you can afford—even with the help of software designed to speed Web authoring. Creating graphics may be similarly time-consuming; fortunately, many word-processing and desktop publishing applications include ready-to-use clip art packages, and you may also incorporate images available for free online in your Web designs. So you have to make intelligent choices, sometimes sticking with technologies you know, at other times exploring new, if more risky, possibilities.

Consider the constraints on your readers, too, when designing your projects. For instance, large electronic files may be time-consuming to download or access on-line. On the WWW, break this complex information into smaller segments, and offer a table of contents or an index page to give readers direct access to the information they need. When a lengthy report might supply more detail than many readers require, include an abstract to summarize the piece, or consider creating a brochure to highlight the most compelling information.

d **Medium.** Your choice of medium will dictate some design considerations. For example, print documents often adhere to traditional formats: they need to be produced with a quality printer (preferably a laser or ink-jet printer), usually on plain white paper with black ink. The fonts and colors you choose will often depend on the capabilities of your printer. Your use of graphics may build, at least in part, on your familiarity with your word processor's capabilities, your proficiency with various text art or drawing programs, and your access to scanners, clip art files, and other equipment. You could include graphics by the old-fashioned cut-and-paste method (literally pasting cutout copies of graphics onto your document pages themselves), but this option is limiting. You'll produce better, more professional documents when you master the intricacies of graphics programs.

For Web projects, you will also have to know how to create and/or incorporate graphics, fonts, hypertext links, and other important elements of page design, making sure all the pieces work together to deliver information to readers. And, of course, you will need to have permission to post your files to an Internet service that allows WWW access.

3.1.2 **Principles of effective document design.** Regardless of the format you choose for a project, you'll find the following principles essential to effective document design.

a **Find a structure appropriate to your project.** Such a structure supports and explains your main point(s). For many projects, you will be expected to follow preexisting structures and patterns. For example, a scientific research report in APA style includes the following parts.

I. Abstract

II. Introduction

III. Method

IV. Results

V. Discussion

Patterns as straightforward as that used for a research report help writers to control their work by suggesting roughly what goes where. Conventional patterns also help readers follow the direction of a project: they look for familiar headings and transitions. For example, in a formal proposal, readers may expect the following issues to be covered.

I. Nature of the Problem

II. Approaches to the Problem

III. Proposal

IV. Feasibility of the Proposal

V. Implications or Conclusion

Even a structure as rudimentary as this one can help you design a project.

I. Introduction

II. Thesis

III. Body

IV. Conclusion

Obviously, you need to understand the conventions of various projects to know whether to follow specific patterns of organization. Even when no such patterns are available, strive for a simple design that highlights key points and suits the medium you've chosen for your work.

b **Lead the reader's eye to important information.**   A basic principle of design is that large chunks of text are hard to read. So break them up. You can often make an essay more approachable simply by dividing it into logical paragraphs or using section headings to mark off chunks of information. On the screen, readers find massive blocks of text especially boring or intimidating. Paragraphs on the WWW (as well as in most brochures and résumés) should be brief.

SET OFF TEXT WITH HEADINGS. Headings are another way to give shape to a project. A short research paper may need only a title. But in longer papers and projects, readers will appreciate subheadings that summarize the content of major sections. All such heads should be brief, parallel in phrasing, and consistent in format—much like the statements in a formal outline. For most academic papers, you will probably use no more than two levels of headings: a title and one set of subheads. For longer works, you may need more. As shown on the next page, headings for an academic paper in MLA style are usually simple; other styles may number paragraph or section headings. See the appropriate style guide for your discipline for more information.

USE LISTS TO SET OFF TEXT. Complicated information or instructions that must be followed in a specific order may be best presented online as either an ordered list (if the instructions must be followed in sequence) or an unordered, or bulleted, list (when the order of operations is not essential). Ordered lists usually use numbers or letters to designate the sequence.

1. Take out two slices of fresh bread.
2. Spread one slice of bread with a thin layer of peanut butter.
3. Spread the other slice of bread with a layer of your favorite jam or jelly.
4. Place the two slices of bread together, coated layers facing each other.
5. Enjoy.

Bulleted lists highlight key ideas that do not require a specific order.

- Use bulleted lists to highlight key ideas that do not require a specific order.

Wilber 7

does not participate or rates the sites
dishonestly.

Filtering Software
    Filtering software such as
CyberSitter and *Net Nanny* is usually
designed to allow users to identify key
words or sites to block. Although this
software can be useful for parents and
schools who are concerned about
children's access to inappropriate
material on the Internet, opponents
argue that many useful sites may also
be blocked. For example, one company
excluded the word "breast" from its
list of accessible words, angering
breast-cancer awareness groups.
    Some sites have made it easier to
identify content on their site by
following the guidelines developed by
the Platform for Internet Content
Selection (PICS). PICS allows sites to

- Use ordered lists to present ideas that must occur in a
  certain sequence.

c **Use graphics and figures as appropriate.**
You should employ graphics when they help readers understand your ideas better than words alone can. Bar
graphs and pie charts, for example, make numbers easier
to interpret and trends more evident. Many word
processors and office suites offer simple templates and
programs for creating figures, charts, and graphs that

can be "dragged and dropped" from one application to another—for instance, from a spreadsheet program to your word-processed document or HTML project.

Learn to use other graphics tools available in word-processing programs or office suites for creating features as simple as columns and boxes. If you have access to the WWW, you can find sites that offer free graphics and other items you can download and incorporate into your print or online projects. Make sure, of course, that you properly acknowledge any such borrowings and adhere to copyright regulations. (For more on citing graphics and other online sources, see Part 4; for more on copyright and fair use, see Section 1.1.)

Be careful not to clutter your work, however. Just because you have easy access to graphics doesn't mean you must illustrate every page. Develop an eye for elegant (meaning "simple") presentations on paper or on screen, and learn to use "white space" in your documents.

d   Use font styles and colors with caution.
Mixing too many font styles or using colors extravagantly can be distracting and unattractive. For most projects, try a simple serif style font such as Times Roman. Use 10- to 12-point type. Fonts that are too large can be as difficult to read as those that are too small. Use a good-quality printer and white paper to increase contrast for easy readability.

e   Plan ahead.
Readers must grasp the logic of your design easily and must be able to find the information they need. Just as you might use scratch outlines to help shape papers, you can prepare preliminary drawings or sketches to explore the design of image-oriented and hyperlinked Web projects (see Section 3.3). You may also need to incorporate navigational aids, such as links or small graphics called icons, to lead readers to important information. For hypertext documents, you may choose to append information that is important but not essential to your focus in separate files linked to your main site.

Font Styles

SERIF FONTS

Serif fonts are the most easily readable. The "feet" lead the reader's eye and help in recognition of letters and words. Use serif fonts for most body text. These are some of the more common serif fonts.

- Courier
- Times or Times New Roman
- Bookman Old Style

SANS SERIF FONTS

Sans serif fonts are generally not as easy to read as serif fonts, but they have a clean look that stands out. Use sans serif fonts for headings. These are examples of common sans serif fonts.

- Arial
- Futura
- Helvetica

Designing Print Documents

Since the invention of movable type in the fifteenth century, people have relied on printed texts for much of their information. Thanks to powerful software and high-speed printers, almost anyone today can produce documents that rival those from a print shop. But many writers have abused this design capability, sometimes forgetting that design should enhance a message, not become the message itself. Fortunately, most professional and academic disciplines offer sensible guidelines for formatting documents. You will want to consult the style guide for your field whenever you begin a major project—whether a paper or something less conventional. You don't want to waste time creating projects you ultimately cannot use.

Checklist for Research Projects

- For academic papers, have you placed your name, your instructor's name, the date, and the course name on the first or title page, if appropriate?
- Is the title centered? Are only the major words and any proper nouns capitalized? (Do not use boldfaced type, underlining, italics, or different font sizes or types for titles.)
- Did you number the pages? Are they in the right order?
- Have you double-spaced your text?
- Are tables and figures labeled correctly and introduced in the text?
- Have you provided transitions and navigational aids such as subheadings, if appropriate?
- Have you used quotation marks and parentheses correctly and in pairs? (The closing quotation mark and parenthesis are often forgotten.)
- Have you indented all direct quotations of four typed lines or more (MLA) or of forty words or more (APA)?
- Have you remembered that indented quotations are not placed between quotation marks?
- Did you introduce all direct quotations with some identification of their author, source, or significance?
- Have you handled titles correctly, italicizing the titles of books and putting the titles of articles between quotation marks?
- Did you include a Works Cited or References page? Is it alphabetized correctly? Did you handle the formatting correctly?
- Have you proofread your work carefully for errors? (Use a spelling checker if available, but carefully proofread your final document as well before declaring it finished.)

3.2.1 **Designing academic papers and essays for final print copy.** Most academic papers are relatively restrained, using diverse fonts, colors, and even graphics only minimally. However, within these limits, academic essays do include specific design criteria you must consider. To format such documents correctly (as shown in Figure 3.1), you will have to use

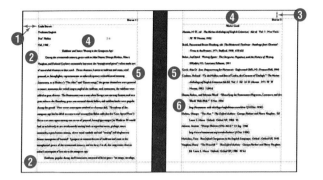

1 1" margins
2 Indent paragraphs 5 spaces or 1/2" using the tab key.
3 1/2"
4 Center titles on page.
5 Double-space throughout.
6 Use automatic hanging-indent feature to format bibliographic entries.

FIGURE 3.1   **Pages from an academic paper formatted according to MLA guidelines.**

standard fonts and font sizes; place titles, bylines, and headings correctly; follow conventions of paragraphing; and, when appropriate, provide proper parenthetical citations, Works Cited pages, and other required elements.

Any graphics and figures you use should enhance or clarify information presented within a text. Don't employ them decoratively in academic papers.

Tables and figures need to be identified. Label a table above the item, spelling out the word *Table*. Refer to both figures or tables in the body of the paper—for example, "See Figure 6." Place a figure caption below the illustration, as in Figure 3.2, abbreviating the word *Figure* to *Fig.*

For an APA paper, check the detailed coverage of tables and figures in the *Publication Manual of the American Psychological Association* (4th ed.).

For the most part, the use of color is inappropriate in academic papers. To emphasize text, use italics rather

TABLE 12	**Economic Dimensions of the Bond Market, 1980–90**		
	YEAR-END AMOUNTS OUTSTANDING (IN BILLIONS)		
TYPE OF ISSUER[a]	1980	1985	1995
U.S. Treasury	$159.8	$427.0	$1,023.6
U.S. agencies	17.6	276.1	447.3
States and municipalities	144.4	322.3	734.9
Corporations	181.0	421.7	752.3
Total	$502.8	$1,447.1	$2,958.1

Sources: Federal Reserve Bulletin, U.S. Treasury Bulletin, and Survey of Current Business.

[a]Excludes institutional issues; data are not available.

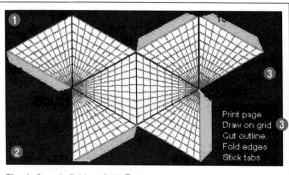

Fig. 1. Generic Foldout Grid ❹

❶ Use figures to illustrate concepts or provide information, not as decoration.
❷ Refer to figures in the body of the text.
❸ Include any necessary explanatory material.
❹ Place the caption below the illustration.

FIGURE 3.2 **A properly prepared table (above) and figure (below). (*Source:* Graphic courtesy of Barry Thomson)**

than boldface characters. Underlining should be avoided in most academic papers since it has become a standard means of designating a hypertext link. This stricture applies even to print documents prepared using newer word processors that automatically reformat

URLs and electronic addresses as hypertext links, usually changing their color and underlining them, as shown here.

http://www.awlonline.com/englishpages

If you are using a black-and-white printer, the link will appear in a shade of gray; otherwise, it will usually print in blue (which is also the default color in many WWW browsers for designating a hypertext link).

Word processors today also enable you to create links to other word-processed documents or to pop-up applications such as Web browsers, spreadsheets, or databases. Many documents are now being distributed and read electronically (on disk or CD-ROM or as email attachments), so these features may be appropriate in your projects. For print, however, files and documents outside the text itself cannot be accessed by the reader unless they are included as appendixes.

Be certain to take advantage of the automatic formatting features of your word processor, such as italics, block indent, hanging indent, page numbering, headers, centering, and so on. Most word processors include built-in help that can make learning these features easier. If necessary, consider taking a course on word processing (perhaps one is offered by your school), or purchase one of the many books available to help you get the most from your software.

3.2.2 **Designing articles for submission in hard copy to publishers.** Publishers of journals and magazines usually have their own submission guidelines, which must be followed meticulously. Most prefer that design elements in manuscripts be kept to a minimum and that authors use few if any of the automatic formatting features available in their word processors. Instead, many publishers require the use of tags to designate features of print documents. The tags tell a printer exactly how to treat various elements.

Columbia Online Style recommends standardized tags to designate common elements of print documents submitted for publication. For example, titles and headings can be designated as follows.

```
<H1>Book Titles</H1>
<H2>Chapter Article Title</H2>
<H3>A-level Heading</H3>
<H4>B-level Heading</H4>
```

Many of the tags recommended by COS are the same tags used to format HTML documents (see Section 3.4), so they can easily be searched and replaced by publishers. For more information, see *The Columbia Guide to Online Style* (Columbia UP, 1998).

Follow the style manual or publisher's guidelines as required for your project, respecting any recommendations about length, margins, spacing, and placement of notes. Make sure your printouts are clean and legible, with margins wide enough to allow for editing. Include separate camera-ready copies of all artwork.

3.2.3 **Designing brochures and newsletters.** Desktop publishing software such as Adobe *PageMaker* and Broderbund *Print Shop* enables you to create brochures and newsletters that rival those from print shops. Many of these programs include templates to convert your files easily to HTML for publication on the Web.

With brochures and newsletters you have more freedom for artistic expression than with academic essays. For example, you can use colors and fonts for visual emphasis and graphics for illustration or decoration. But some design principles will constrain you. You usually want a design that leads a reader's eye between important elements. So make sure that the headings in a brochure are in the right order, that the various sections follow in correct sequence when the brochure is folded, and that the panels contain all pertinent information, especially phone numbers and addresses. In newsletters, try to place stories so that headlines don't "bump," remember to balance the elements on a page, and use boxes and shading to highlight key features. Avoid large blocks of text in both brochures and newsletters; too much type intimidates readers. And don't use too many colors—they can be distracting, and they are expensive to reproduce in items printed commercially.

Consider, too, such matters as the size of the paper, the number of folds, whether to leave space for mailing addresses on your document, whether you will use text art or clip art images, and whether you will create your own graphics or scan in photographs or artwork. If you will be printing the item yourself, the size of the computer file for your brochure or newsletter may not be important; however, if you need to save your work on a disk or in another medium, make certain that the file size does not exceed the capacity of your storage medium, and verify that the print shop or publisher can handle the format you use.

Many word-processing and desktop publishing applications offer templates for brochures and newsletters as well as other types of documents, as shown in Figure 3.3. These templates can guide you in layout and design while still allowing you a great deal of creativity. For more information on using templates, check the help file or manual for your software package.

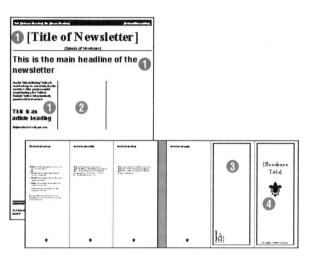

❶ Preset heading definitions help the reader locate information.
❷ A newsletter template uses columns to lay out text and graphics.
❸ One panel of the brochure is reserved for the address of the recipient.
❹ Use your own graphics, colors, and fonts to customize the brochure.

FIGURE 3.3 Use templates to help format difficult projects.
(*Source: Corel WordPerfect 6.1 for Windows*)

3.2.4 Designing business and technical reports and documents.

When designing business and technical reports and documents, you usually can use graphics, including photographic images, graphs, and tables. Some reports, such as corporate annual reports or sales documents, may incorporate full-color reproductions, photographs, and other complex graphical elements. These reports may be costly and have to be

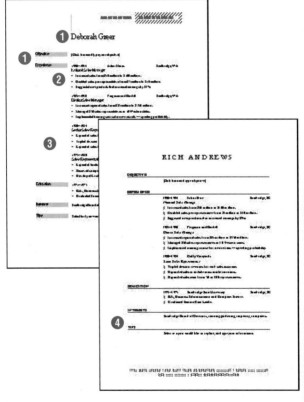

1. Use different fonts or type styles to set off information.
2. Use columns or tables without borders to help align information.
3. Use white space to lead the eye to important information.
4. Templates can help ensure that you don't omit important information.

FIGURE 3.4 Use templates to help make your résumé attractive and professional. (*Source:* Corel *WordPerfect 6.1 for Windows*)

professionally printed. Thus, most business and technical documents use color sparingly, if at all.

Readers will find your business documents easy to read if you use features such as headings or section numbers, lists, and tables to highlight important information. You might also include a table of contents or an abstract that summarizes important information. Use graphics to illustrate key concepts and processes.

When you prepare a résumé, use a conservative design for most job applications. (The exception might be if you are applying for a position in an artistic capacity, such as for an advertising agency.) In many word processors, you can find templates like those shown in Figure 3.4 to guide you through the creation of attractive résumés. The software may suggest what items of information you should include and may even suggest appropriate language strategies (for example, using action verbs).

Designing Electronic Documents

When you need to produce a professional document today, you'll likely create it in an electronic format. You'll design many documents in versatile text-editing programs such as Microsoft *Word* or Corel *WordPerfect*; you may use a desktop publishing program to create forms, newsletters, and other print documents. You might illustrate a lecture or a group presentation with slides or handouts prepared on software such as *PowerPoint*. If you are developing a Web site, you'll rely on HTML editors and other kinds of design software. Gradually, you will gain experience with a surprising range of electronic tools for shaping documents.

Some of these documents may be read online only, a trend likely to accelerate. For example, you may already be in a course in which most class materials, including syllabi and policy statements, are distributed online only. Some colleges and universities are involved in the Networked Digital Library of Theses and Dissertations (NDLTD), part of an initiative to publish electronic versions of theses and dissertations on the WWW; some of the institutions involved are no longer publishing printed copies of these works at all.

Luckily, you can easily translate many of the principles of good document design from print to electronic forms of publication. Readers always appreciate clear headings, lots of white space, and a logical flow of ideas. However, some new guidelines for electronic media have evolved in response to the needs of writers and readers, and other conventions simply no longer apply to works on screen. For example, double spacing and hanging indents, while a staple of most academic papers, are quickly becoming anachronisms in HTML publications.

Checklist for Good Document Design

- Make sure all hypertext links are working. For external links, you may want to include a list describing each link in case the intended file moves or is changed.
- Make sure your graphics print or load accurately and quickly.
- Check the appearance of your work carefully. For WWW documents and files, try a variety of browsers; for documents to be read using electronic means, make sure files will transfer across platforms or applications. For print documents, include a header with your last name or title of the work (as appropriate) and the page number.
- Include bibliographical information: your name and a way to contact you (e.g., your email address) if appropriate, the title of your work or site, the date of creation or last modification, and the URL for the site if it is on the WWW.
- Give credit in the proper format to any sources you have borrowed from, including the source of any graphics.

The guidelines we present here are admittedly tentative, a fusion of old and new principles. But they should help you adapt your documents aesthetically to the demands of purpose, audience, and context you face whenever you work in electronic formats.

3.3.1 **Electronic correspondence (email).** Many people are now using point-and-click editors that make it possible to include colors, fonts, graphics, links, and multimedia elements in the body of email messages. But the standard for electronic mail is still ASCII (American Standard Code for Information Interchange) text—which does not allow for special formatting or automatic links. Any graphics or multimedia elements must be downloaded and read using separate applications. The same is true of email attachments, which must also be downloaded and opened with appropriate software. So here's an important guideline: When you attach files to email, be sure they are in formats accessible to your readers. Remember that what you send from your end is not necessarily how your readers will see it at theirs.

Of course, your email and online documents should adhere to many of the same principles that apply to print documents. However, there are additional considerations when you write electronically.

a **Be considerate.** Electronic files can be large, especially when they incorporate forwarded messages or a string of replies to an initial posting. Not only can such files be time-consuming for your reader, but they can use up valuable resources, contributing to "lag" on the Internet. Some readers may even incur additional fees to download large files. So when you reply to a posting, quote only relevant portions of the original message; it is rarely necessary to include the entire series of messages to which you are responding. Do not attach graphics or multimedia files just because you have that capability; make sure you really need to send them. And do not forward chain mail or "spam" unless you are quite sure your reader enjoys these types of messages.

b **Use ASCII characters to indicate text formatting.** ASCII does not allow a writer to use italics, underlining, or boldface characters in a message, but conventions have emerged online to convey these features. You may need them to highlight titles or show emphasis.

- Use the underscore character (_) before and after a word or phrase to indicate text that would be underlined or italicized in print (_The Scarlet Letter_).

- Use asterisks (*) to indicate text that might be boldfaced in print (ASCII does *not* provide for the use of boldfaced fonts).

- Use asterisks or tags and emoticons (ASCII characters used to designate facial expressions) to convey emotions if appropriate. For example, a sideways smiley face :) indicates humor; asterisks may surround a word to express emotion (*grin*); and some writers surround text with "tags" to explain their meaning (<SARCASM>). The text between these tags is meant to be sarcastic</SARCASM>.

c **Follow guidelines for proper netiquette.** In online conversations, it can be easy to misread a writer's intentions because we lack the cues of face-to-face interactions. So etiquette is as important online as it is off, perhaps even more so. For advice about online etiquette, or netiquette, see Section 2.3.

3.3.2 **Files to be read online.** Many electronic files, including some word-processed documents, are designed to be read online rather than in print. These files often include "embedded" applications, that is, links to read-only versions of other files, programs, or sites—such as spreadsheets or Web browsers. A printed document cannot replicate the movement made possible by such links.

But even with documents meant for print, you should consider what happens when they are being transmitted electronically. How can you be sure readers will be able to use a file? One way is by saving a version of your document as ASCII, RTF (Rich Text Format), or WP5.1 for DOS files. (In most applications, click on "File" then "Save As" and then choose the appropriate file type.) Readers should be able to access files in these formats, whether you create them on disk or transmit them via email or the World Wide Web. Use standard 3.5-inch high-density IBM-formatted floppy diskettes and DOS file-naming conventions, choosing eight-character file names with no spaces, followed by a period and the three-letter extension that designates the type of file. Most applications will automatically add the correct file extension. (See Section 1.3 for more on file extensions.) For example, you might name a file *homepage.htm* or *essay.txt*. Windows95 and 98 and Macintosh users can use longer file names and file extensions (for example, *workscited.html*), but, since these longer names may not translate across platforms, you will need to make certain that your reader can handle them.

3.3.3   **Designing articles for electronic submission to publishers.**   Most publishers require that a standard word-processing package such as *Word* or *WordPerfect* be used to submit articles. Special formatting should be kept to a minimum. Separate larger documents into discrete files: save each chapter of a book-length work as a separate file, and save large graphics as separate files. Manuscripts are usually double spaced throughout and include headers with page numbering and author or title information. For detailed information on creating, saving, and submitting files electronically for print as well as for electronic publication, see *The Columbia Guide to Online Style*.

3.3.4   **Designing articles and forms for electronic publication in PDF formats.**   PDF, or portable document format, files are created using Adobe's *Distiller* program and allow for the creation of electronic files that retain all special formatting, graphics, links, keyword searching, mathematical or scientific notation, and other special features of print documents, regardless of the type of computer the reader is using to access the files. These files can be stored online, accessed electronically, and read using the free Adobe *Acrobat Reader* available for downloading at http://www .adobe.com/prodindex/acrobat/readstep.html. However, the files can be quite large, and they must be downloaded by the user, who must have access to *Acrobat Reader* in order to view them. Because users may not be able to edit them, PDF files should not be used for work that is being shared, such as with publishers. However, PDF files are extremely useful for making advertising material, special forms, or technical documents available electronically, and the NDLTD (see p. 102) uses PDF for online publication of theses and dissertations. (See Virginia Polytechnic Institute's pilot site on electronic theses and dissertations at http://etd.vt.edu/ index.htm for more information.)

3.3.5 **Designing   presentations.**   Programs such as Corel *Presentations* and Microsoft *PowerPoint* make it easy even for beginners to produce professional-quality electronic presentations. Many of these can also be published on the WWW. Figure 3.5 includes streaming video and audio (that is, files that can be played while they are downloading, thus saving the annoying waiting time that often plagues large files) as well as "slides." The viewer can read along with the text and can control the speed and volume of the presentation, skip through slides to access key points, or sit back and enjoy the show. However, when you prepare a presentation, you will need to make sure your audience has access to the necessary software to view these files or that you will have the equipment needed to project your presentation.

In many presentations, you will use slides to convey information in outline form to a live audience. Beginners often make the mistake of providing too much or too little information on a slide. You ordinarily need a title and a few bulleted points on each slide—enough to keep the audience interested and on track. Crowd too much information on a slide, and you will distract viewers and may make the slide hard to read: it is up to you to provide the details orally. Offer too little information, and the slide will seem irrelevant, maybe even distracting.

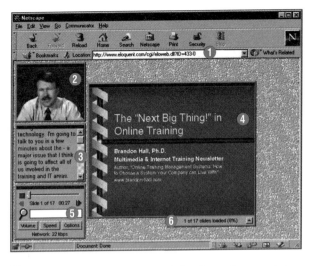

① Plug-in applications display presentations in your browser window.

② Streaming video brings the presentation to life.

③ Scrolling text display allows the viewer to read along.

④ Slides use text and graphics to highlight key points.

⑤ Users control the volume and speed of the audio file.

⑥ New slides load automatically; users can move forward or backward in the presentation.

FIGURE 3.5   **Presentation software can include audio and video files.** (*Source:* Brandon Hall, "The 'Next Big Thing!' in Online Training," http://www.eloquent.com/cgi/eloweb .dll?ID=433-0)

For your slides, you can choose both varied font sizes and colors. Begin by considering the size of the room in which you will make your presentation and the projection equipment you will need. For electronic presentations, you may want to consider using sans serif fonts (see p. 93); use a size large enough to be read easily, and use high contrast (white backgrounds and dark text or dark backgrounds with light text) for easy visibility. Use graphics or multimedia elements and colors with care—make sure they are important to your presentation and do not distract your audience's attention from what you have to say. Always test your slides to be certain they are readable by your audience. Also proofread them carefully—your audience will have plenty of time to spot glaring errors! (For more on designing effective

presentations, see http://www.presentingsolutions.com/
effectivepresentations.html or http://www.eloquent.com.)

3.3.6 **Designing WWW projects.** Perhaps
the most important and yet most often overlooked step
in designing a project for the World Wide Web is plan-
ning. Using paper and pencil, sketch out a proposed layout, indicating links, navigational features, graphics,
headings, and other elements you would like to include
in your design. Think about what users will be looking
for in the site, and plan how you can get them to the information they need. Keep the design simple. Remember, too, that your initial design may (and probably
will) change considerably as you actually compose your
pages, so be flexible. Consider alternatives to your design in case you come up against design constraints imposed by limits on your technical knowledge, your access to programs and resources, or your time. In short,
be realistic.

Other principles of good document design for the
WWW to consider are discussed below.

a **Use contrast for easy readability.** Most
print documents are best read using a white background
and black print. On the WWW, contrast is also an important consideration. Use background graphics and
colors with caution; choose fonts and font sizes that enhance readability. Although it may be possible to set
fonts and colors that cannot be overridden by the
reader, in many instances the WWW author does not
know what changes a reader can make to a document's
format (sometimes the reader doesn't even know).
Thus, you may waste your time incorporating fancy elements that distract readers from the message you want
to convey.

b **Break up large blocks of text.** Keep paragraphs short on WWW pages. Use headings and subheads as appropriate to move the reader's eye to important information. Use white space (blank areas) to
provide contrast and legibility. To see these principles
in action, study pages on the WWW that you find especially readable.

c **Use graphics or other design elements sparingly.** Graphics must be appropriate. They can be used to attract the reader's attention to important information (for example, an email icon may alert the reader to information on contacting the author) or for navigational purposes (image maps, "Back" buttons, and other graphical elements can aid the reader in moving through the document). However, a page full of animated graphics and blinking text will probably just give your reader eyestrain and detract from what you have to say.

d **Include a table of contents, page anchors, or other navigational aids.** Like printed texts, hypertext pages such as those you read on the WWW need transitional devices. Some of those transitions—such as titles, headings, and numerical sequences—are familiar because they are part of most texts, whether printed or electronic. But hypertext also offers many special devices. For example, you can use page anchors (links to specific sections of a Web page) to scroll readers through lengthy online documents or establish hypertext links to move them from page to page or document to document. You can create arrows, image maps (see Section 3.4), or buttons to provide graphical transitions or use pop-up browser windows for digressions or explanations. Use all these devices to be sure readers always know where they are in your material and how to get where they need to be.

e **Include bibliographical information in your electronic document.** Provide your reader with all the information necessary to cite your document and (when necessary) to contact you for permission to use your material. Essential bibliographical information includes the following elements.

1. Your name and email address or email link.
2. Title of your work.
3. Date of publication/creation and/or date of last modification or revision.
4. URL for your document and/or your home page.

In their "Draft Guidelines for Providing Web-Site Information" at http://www.english.ohio-state.edu/People/Ulman.1/guidelines/Web_guidelines.htm, MLA recommends that you also include information on your site's sponsor, purpose, software requirements, site configuration, and other useful information.

f **Give credit to your sources.**   Include the source of any graphics or other files you used in your document. Don't just provide a link to an online source; always include full bibliographical information, or at least the URL of the source, in your text. Then people who print out your document from the WWW won't lose track of the linked sources—which may print out only as underscored words or phrases. (See Section 1.1 for more information on copyright and ethics.)

g **Make your site accessible.**   Not everyone has access to the latest hardware and software applications, so you should design your Web pages with such limitations in mind. If the size of your site might cause problems for people downloading it, consider limiting file sizes by including "thumbnail" (reduced-size) images or text descriptions on your pages with links to large multimedia files. Or you might treat interesting but unnecessary material, explanations, or definitions as separate linked files. If your readers might need to download special software plug-ins to access your work, provide the necessary links. Be aware that items such as graphics, frames, and tables may not be readable across different computer platforms. So consider including text-only versions of documents and verbal descriptions of graphic or audio files that some site users might not be able to access. These considerations may also make your work more accessible to people with impaired vision or hearing or to non-English-speaking people as well. For more information, see "Making Web Pages Universally Accessible" by Sheryl Burgstahler in CMC *Magazine* at http://www.december.com/cmc/mag/1998/jan/burg.html or the WWW Consortium's "Web Content Accessibility Guidelines 1.0" at http://www.w3.org/TR/1999/WAI-WEBCONTENT-19990505/.

Putting Together a Basic Web Page

Many students already have a Web page; if you don't, you can quickly and easily learn to create one. There are many excellent Web authoring tools that can simplify what may seem to be a daunting task, and many word processors now allow you to save your work automatically in HTML format for Web publication. Using a graphical Web editor such as Netscape's *Composer* or Microsoft's *FrontPage*, you can design a Web page with point-and-click ease, or you can use any number of powerful text-based HTML editors to include even advanced features in your designs with ease. You can also try *Web Page Wizard* at http://www.netscape.com/assist/net_sites/starter/wizard/index.html. However, you don't need any special tools to begin creating a Web page. You can use a simple text editor such as *Notepad*, available in most Windows platforms, or an online editor such as *Pico* to get started.

3.4.1   **A basic template.**   Many WWW authoring programs include a selection of templates, and as you learn more about HTML authoring, you can design your own. To get started quickly, you can copy the quick start template on page 112 into your text or HTML editor. The information shown in **blue** on the template should be replaced with your own information. Figure 3.6 shows how this page will appear on the World Wide Web. To see your own page, save the file with an .htm or .html extension, then open it in your Web browser. (For more information, see Section 3.4.5.)

Note that ISO Latin1 characters "©" are used to include the copyright symbol (see Fig. 3.6, p. 113).

3.4.2   **Designing your Web site.**   Web pages offer a great deal of flexibility in design. But just as a traditional essay must follow a logical structure, a Web site

Quick Start Template

```
<HTML>
<HEAD>
  <TITLE>Title of Your Site</TITLE>

  <META NAME="Author" CONTENT="Your Name">
  <META NAME="Title" CONTENT="Title of Your
  Page">
  <META NAME="Date of Creation" CONTENT="Day
  Month Year">
  <META NAME="URL" CONTENT="http://your
  .address.edu">
</HEAD>

<BODY>
<H1>Title on Your Page</H1>
<A HREF="mailto:your_email_address">Your
Name</A1>
<HR>

<P>Insert your text here. You may want to use lists,
tables, or other features to help you format your
page.</P>

<P>You can also insert graphics, links, and other
elements as appropriate.</P>

<HR>
<FONT SIZE="-1">&copy; Your Name<BR>
Date of Creation or Last Modification: Day Month
Year<BR>
URL for this page: http://your.address.edu
</FONT>

</BODY>
</HTML>
```

needs a coherent system of organization. The "Yale
C/AIM Web Style Guide" at http://info.med.yale.edu/
caim/manual/ defines four basic structures: a linear sequence, a gridwork structure, a hierarchical structure,
and a hub or network structure. The design you choose
will depend on your purpose and audience as well as on
the nature of the information you are presenting.

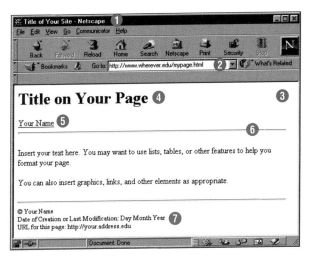

1. Information enclosed between the <TITLE> and </TITLE> tags appears in the browser information bar.
2. URL for your home page
3. The body of your file appears in the browser window.
4. The title of your page is formatted as a level one header.
5. Your name is formatted as an email link.
6. Horizontal rules are used to separate sections of the page.
7. Bibliographic information about the page

FIGURE 3.6   A basic Web page template.

a   A linear sequence.   Many Web sites follow a simple, linear sequence. For shorter works, your site may consist of a single page with headings and subheadings to help the reader locate important information and to draw the reader through the page. (See Section 3.1 for more on headings.) For longer, more complicated projects, you may want to include an index or table of contents with links to the different parts of your page or to additional pages within your site. You may also want to include "Next" and "Back" links on each page.

b   A gridwork design.   A more complicated structure might begin with an index page that has links to additional pages which, in turn, link to other pages. Such a pattern forms a kind of gridwork and is useful for presenting information that depends on previous information but does not necessarily follow a linear sequence. Online help manuals for software applications usually follow such a pattern, allowing the reader to connect to related ideas; the process is similar to cross-referencing in an encyclopedia or another reference work. In addition to linking pages to related information, you should include links back to the main index page to help keep your reader from getting lost.

c **A hierarchical structure.**   Sometimes information is dependent on other information. That is, it is necessary to understand one part before moving to another. You can construct such a hierarchical structure by connecting your pages to each other following a format similar to a genealogical or organizational chart. Information presented in this format follows a top-down structure, with branches to show relationships between related parts at the same level. Again, make sure each page includes a "Back" link to the main index page or to the beginning of each branch so your reader doesn't follow the links to a dead end.

d **A hub or network design.**   Sites may also radiate from a central "hub" with spokes (or links) connecting each page to every other page, forming a web or network. This kind of structure works best for information that is interrelated: that is, all parts are related to each other and to the whole but are not dependent on each other. This structure allows the reader to access the information in any order. One way to create such a site is to include your pages inside a frame (a way of dividing the browser window into two or more sections). The frame remains on the screen at all times while other pages appear inside the frame. Keep in mind, however, that not all browsers support frames; another method that may ensure greater accessibility is simply to link each page in your site back to a main index page.

Figure 3.7 shows a site designed using frames. To make the site more accessible, the designer offers readers a choice of entering the site using either the frames version or a text-only version without frames. The menu bar on the left side of the page is the frame, with

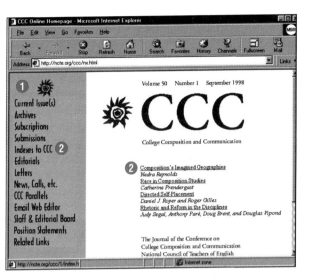

1 A menu bar on the frame offers readers access to links.
2 Linked pages appear inside the frame.

FIGURE 3.7   **A page designed using frames.** (*Source:* **Home page, *CCC*, http://ncte.org/ccc/nx.html**)

links to other pages within the site appearing in the browser window inside the frame. Thus, the reader always has ready access to the links on the menu bar.

3.4.3   Creating a table of contents.   Unless your site consists of only one page, no more than one or two screens in length, you will probably want to include an index (or table of contents) page with links to other parts of your page or to other pages within your site. Figure 3.8 shows some different ways to format a table of contents or index page. Keep in mind, however, that your reader must be able to access the information you provide, so using graphics or advanced techniques (such as the pull-down menu shown in Figure 3.8) might limit who will be able to read your site. The format you choose should make sense for your purpose and audience and should clearly lead the reader to important information. That said, however, a little creativity can go a long way toward making your site attractive and appealing to readers without sacrificing clarity and accessibility.

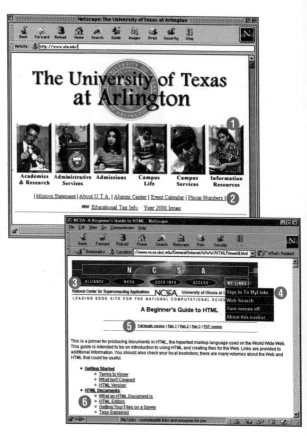

① Graphics with text descriptions link to additional pages within the Web site.

② Text-only menu bar links to more Web pages.

③ A graphic formatted as an image map; areas of the image link to various sites

④ Pull-down menus link to specific Web pages within the site.

⑤ Text-only menu bar offers a choice of formats, making the site more accessible across various platforms.

⑥ Text links use an outline format to show relationships. Links are to name references or to designated sections of the same Web page.

FIGURE 3.8 Formatting a table of contents or index page. (*Sources:* Home page, University of Texas at Arlington, http://www.uta.edu/index.old.html; and NCSA, "A Beginner's Guide to HTML," http://www.ncsa.uiuc.edu/General/Internet/WWW/HTMLPrimerAll.html)

Using the quick start template below, you can create a simple table of contents with links to additional pages in your site. Information shown in **blue** should be replaced with your own information. For example, replace **intro.html** with the name of the file to which you want to link, and replace **Introduction** with the page heading or title to which you are linking.

Quick Start Template

<H2>Table of Contents</H2>

<A HREF="intro.html">Introduction</A>
<A HREF="start.html">Getting Started</A>
<A HREF="structure.html">Deciding on a Structure</A>

Create *name references* to link to other parts of the same page by inserting the tags <A NAME="**name**"> and </A> immediately before the text or section to which you want to link. In the table of contents, replace the file name with the name reference preceded by a pound sign (#), for example, <A HREF="#**name**">**Name**</A>. You can also create links to external sites, that is, links to other pages or sites on the WWW, by including the complete address for the desired target. For example, to link to the Web site for this book, include the tags <A HREF="**http://www.awlonline.com/researchcentral/**">**Research Central**</A> in your template.

3.4.4   **The parts of an HTML document.** An HTML document consists of two primary parts: the *head,* which defines the elements of the page, and the *body,* which defines the structure of the page. The <HEAD> includes such elements as the <TITLE> and the <META> tags (see the quick start template on p. 112). The information in the head of the document will not appear on your page itself; the <TITLE> information appears in the bar at the top of your browser and is used by many search engines to find information online. This title should be as descriptive as possible and should not include any formatting information or special characters. Metatags provide content information that is used by many search engines and accessible by viewing the source code of a page. Although content information is not required, providing some (for example, the author's name, the site title, and the date of creation) can ensure that readers have information necessary to evaluate and cite sources they find on the WWW.

The <BODY> tag in your template is used to define the structure of the page itself, allowing you to designate various attributes, such as background colors or graphics or text and link colors for your document. The sections that follow give advice and examples to help get you started. For more information, see the NCSA site *The Beginner's Guide to HTML* at http://www.ncsa.uiuc.edu/General/Internet/WWW/HTML_Primer.html.

a Formatting text.   One of the things that makes HTML so useful for publication of documents and files is its ability to include document structure tags, that is, tags that change the appearance of the document, allowing you to create headings, emphasize (or de-emphasize) text, or add other useful features. Many Web page authoring programs simplify this process by offering menus or buttons with common formatting options. Some newer word processors also translate common text formatting into HTML automatically. (See your program's help file for more information.) If you are using a text-based editor, you can use the HTML tags shown in Figure 3.9 and Table 3.1 (p.120) to get started.

In the quick start template on page 112, you may have noticed that the title of your page was enclosed in <H1> and </H1> tags, which formatted the title as large, dark text. These tags denote a header and are used to set off sections of text in your document. (See Section 3.2 for more on using headings.) HTML allows for six levels of headers, as shown in Figure 3.9.

You can also indicate emphasis by changing the appearance of the text on the reader's screen. For example, you can show text in **boldface type,** *italic type,* or

<H1>Level One Header</H1>

<H2>Level Two Header</H2>

<H3>Level Three Header</H3>

<H4>Level Four Header</H4>

<H5>Level Five Header</H5>

<H6>Level Six Header</H6>

FIGURE 3.9   Headers in HTML.

even *boldface italic type* simply by enclosing it within the proper tags. Using the <FONT> and </FONT> tags, you can also change the font size, typeface (e.g., Times New Roman, Helvetica), or color. In the quick start template on page 112, the copyright statement, the date of creation, and the URL shown at the bottom of the page appear slightly smaller than preceding text because these items are enclosed between the <FONT SIZE="–1"> and </FONT> tags.

Spacing (other than a single space between words), line breaks, tabs, and other such formatting in your documents will not show up on the Web unless you include HTML tags to define these attributes as well. Table 3.1 shows some commonly used HTML tags for formatting text, spacing, and other elements of your Web page.

b **Using colors and graphics.**   Graphics and colors on your pages should make a statement—they are part of the message you convey. Use them to enhance the readability and visual attractiveness of your page, of course, but make sure they also serve a definite purpose. Pages with too many graphics, or with several animated graphics, not only may take too long to load in a browser but may also appear cluttered and interfere with your primary purpose: to communicate an idea or information to your reader. You can create your own graphics with a scanner, a simple tool such as Windows *Paintbrush,* or a more advanced graphics program such as Corel *Draw* or Adobe *Photoshop.* A wide variety of

TABLE 3.1 **Formatting Text in HTML**
HTML TAG
<STRONG> and </STRONG> or <B> and </B>
<EM> and </EM> or <I> and </I>
<FONT SIZE="**-1**"> and </FONT>
<FONT SIZE="**+1**"> and </FONT>
<FONT COLOR="#**FF0000**"> and </FONT>

<P> and </P>
<CENTER> and </CENTER>
<HR>

background images are available free on the WWW. (See Section 1.1 for information on copyright and the WWW.)

Within the <BODY> tags, you can define various attributes of the entire page, such as the background color or image, text and link colors, fonts, and so forth, or you can change the attributes for specific portions of your document. Graphics-based authoring programs make it easy to add colors and graphics to your page, but if you are using a text-based HTML authoring tool such as *Notepad,* you can simply insert the HTML tags into the

RESULTS	USE
Boldface text	Strong emphasis; headings
Italic text	Emphasis; foreign words; book and journal titles
Reduced font size	Notes
Enlarged font size	Emphasis
Font Color	Emphasis; warnings or safety information
Forces a line break. Text begins on the next line.	End a line
Forces a paragraph break. Text begins on the second line following.	Separate paragraphs of text or other elements
Forces a blank space.	Include blank spaces
Centers elements.	Center text, graphics, tables, or other elements
Places a horizontal rule (or line) on your page.	Separate sections of a document

body of your document as shown in Figure 3.10, replacing the information in the tags with your own design.

c **Using lists and tables.**   Like most word processors and desktop publishing applications, HTML uses special codes to format bulleted (or unordered) lists, numbered (or ordered) lists, definition lists, and tables. (For more on using lists, see Section 3.1.2.) These features allow you a great deal of flexibility in designing your Web page. Lists and tables can be "nested"; that is, you can create a list inside a list or a table within a

122   Part 3   Designing Your Project

table. You can create tables with or without borders, specify the size of cells, and add background graphics or other elements by using HTML tags to define the attributes you want. Tables can be used to simulate columns of text, to help align lists, to decrease download time for

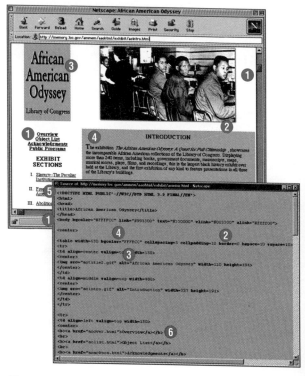

① Change the background and text colors by defining the attributes in the <BODY> tag.
② Use tables without borders to lay out text and graphics on the page.
③ ALT ("alternative") tags describe graphics for text-only browsers.
④ Define background colors for tables.
⑤ Comment lines in the source code begin with an exclamation point (!) and provide information only.
⑥ Links to file and images in the same directory use relative addressing. To link to files and images outside your own directory, include the full URL.

FIGURE 3.10   Adding background colors and graphics.
(Source: Library of Congress, "African American Odyssey" home page and HTML code, http://memory.loc.gov/ammem/ aaohtml/exhibit/aointro.html)

large graphics, or to present data like a spreadsheet. Taking the time to play with these powerful features is well worth the effort.

Web editors like Netscape's *Composer* or Userland Software's *BBEdit* for Macintosh make it easy to include lists and tables in your page. Keep in mind, however, that many text-based browsers and some older graphical browsers cannot handle tables, so the information you format with these tags may look different to some readers. (See also "Making Web Pages Universally Accessible" at http://www.december.com/cmc/mag/1998/jan/burg.html.)

Create lists and tables as shown in Figure 3.11 using the template on p. 124.

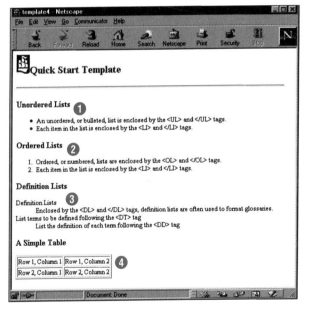

❶ Use unordered (or bulleted) lists to present items of equal importance.

❷ Use ordered (or numbered) lists to present information that requires a certain order.

❸ Use definition lists to format entries in glossaries.

❹ Use tables with borders to simulate the appearance of a spreadsheet or form; use tables without borders to locate text and graphics on a Web page.

FIGURE 3.11 **Formatting lists and tables in HTML.**

Quick Start Template

UNORDERED LISTS
```
<UL>
<LI>An unordered, or bulleted, list is enclosed by the
<UL> and </UL> tags.</LI>
<LI>Each item in the list is enclosed by the <LI> and
</LI> tags.</LI>
</UL>
```

ORDERED LISTS
```
<OL>
<LI>Ordered, or numbered, lists are enclosed by the
<OL> and </OL> tags.</LI>
<LI>Each item in the list is enclosed by the <LI> and
</LI> tags.</LI>
</OL>
```

DEFINITION LISTS
```
<DL>
<DT>Definition Lists
<DD>Enclosed by the <DL> and </DL> tags, definition
lists are often used to format glossaries.
<DT>List terms to be defined following the <DT> tag.
<DD>List the definition for each term following the
<DD> tag.
</DL>
```

TABLES
```
<TABLE BORDER="1">
<TR>
<TD>Row 1, Column 1</TD>
<TD>Row 1, Column 2</TD>
</TR>
<TR>
<TD>Row 2, Column 1</TD>
<TD>Row 2, Column 2</TD>
</TR>
</TABLE>
```

3.4.5 **Publishing your project on the Web.**
When you are ready to publish your page on the
WWW, you will need to transfer, or upload, your files
from your disk or hard drive (your *local host*) to your Internet server (your *remote host*). Many HTML editors

automate this process, but you may need to use an FTP client program. If you don't have an FTP client or don't know how to use the one you have, check with your Internet service provider for instructions.

Many ISPs allow space for WWW pages on their servers, and some sites on the Internet, such as *GeoCities*, offer free Web space to individuals. Your school may also allow space for students to publish home pages. Check with your provider or university computing service for details, and be sure to follow any posted requirements carefully.

Before you publish your pages, however, you will want to see how they will look online. To view your file, first save it, choosing the type of file (such as HTML) and a name. If you are using an application that does not offer .html as a choice of file type, choose ASCII or MS-DOS text, and include the file extension after the file name (for example, *index.html*). You may want to follow DOS file-naming conventions to ensure compatibility across programs and platforms: use an eight-character file name, with no spaces, followed by a period and a three-letter file extension (for example, *index.htm*). Windows95 or 98 and Macintosh users can use longer file names and extensions, but make certain that your Internet server can handle them.

After you have saved your file, open a browser such as Netscape *Navigator* or *Internet Explorer;* click on "File" in the menu bar at the top of your browser, and then choose "Open." Locate your file on your disk or hard drive. You do not need to be connected to the Internet to view your page, but if you view pages offline you may not be able to check links or see some of the graphics.

The checklist on the next page offers some guidelines to consider in reviewing your Web page.

For More Information

Deciding on Format

Bookmarks on the Web
http://www.awlonline.com/researchcentral/

Longman *The English Pages*
http://www.awlonline.com/englishpages/

Checklist for
Good Document Design

- Make sure all hypertext links are working. For external links, you may want to include a list describing each link in case the intended files move or change.
- Make sure your graphics load accurately and quickly. For larger files, consider using thumbnail images or text descriptions with links to the larger file.
- Check the appearance of your work carefully, using different Web browsers if possible. Make sure the file is readable in both text-only and graphical browsers if appropriate.
- Include bibliographical information: your name and a way to contact you (e.g., your email address) if appropriate, the title of your work or site, the date of creation or last modification, and the URL for the site.
- Give credit in the proper format to any sources from which you have borrowed material, including the sources for any graphics or other files you have used.
- If you are including graphics or other material downloaded or copied from outside sources, make certain you have permission to use those materials.
- Try checking your site using the *Web Site Garage* at http://websitegarage.com and *Bobby* at http://cast.org/bobby to make sure your pages are accurate and accessible to disabled users. (For more information, see Sheryl Burgstahler's online article "Making Web Pages Universally Accessible.")

University of Missouri "Online Writery"
http://www.missouri.edu/~writery/

Purdue University's "Online Writing Lab"
http://owl.english.purdue.edu/

The HTML Writer's Guild
http://www.hwg.org/

"The Web Developer's Forum"
http://www.WDVL.com/WDVL/Forum/

Yale Center for Advanced Instructional Media
http://info.med.yale.edu/caim/

Jakob Nielsen's *Usable Information Technology*
http://www.useit.com/

The World Wide Web Consortium
http://www.w3.org/

The Electronic Frontier Foundation
http://www.eff.org/

Library of Congress "HTML"
http://lcweb.loc.gov/global/internet/html.htm

NCSA's *A Beginner's Guide to HTML*
http://www.ncsa.uiuc.edu/General/Internet/WWW/

HyperText Markup Language

The Bare Bones Guide to HTML
http://werbach.com/barebones/barebone.html

"Interactive HTML Tutorial"
**http://www.coedu.usf.edu/inst_tech/
publications/html/**

"HTML Primers: The Basics"
http://www.htmlgoodies.com/primers/basics.htm/

Media Builder's "HTML Editors"
http://www.mediabuilder.com/softwarewebedit.html

Microsoft's *Front Page*
http://www.microsoft.com/frontpage/

Netscape's *Composer*
**http://home.netscape.com/communicator/
composer/**

Apple Computer's "Internet Publishing"
**http://www.apple.com/publishing/internet/
index.html**

Userland Software's *BBEdit* for Macintosh
http://www.scripting.com/bbEdit/

Web Page Design

Yale C/AIM *Web Style Guide*
http://info.med.yale.edu/caim/manual/

Sun *Guide to Web Style*
**http://www.sun.com/styleguide/tables/
Welcome.html**

W3C *Style Guide for Online Hypertext*
http:/www.w3.org/Provider/Style/

"Composing Good HTML"
http://www.cs.cmu.edu/~tilt/cgh

Formatting Elements of Your Page

"ASCII Coded Character Set for HTML"
**http://forum.swarthmore.edu/workshops/usi/
sandiego/ascii.html**

"Character Formatting"
**http://www.ncsa.uiuc.edu/General/Internet/
WWW/HTMLPrimerAll.html#CF**

The HTML Writer's Guild
http://www.hwg.org/

C/Net's "Elements of Web Design"
http://builder.cnet.com/Graphics/Design/

WDVL's "Web Design—More than Meets the Eye"
http://www.WDVL.com/Authoring/Design

A+ Art
http://www.aplusart.com/

"Controlling Document Backgrounds"
http://www.netscape.com/assist/net_sites/bg/

maranGraphic's "Web Color Chart"
http://www.maran.com/colorchart/index.html

Joe Barta's *Table Tutor*
http://www.fix.net/~wmiller/tabletutor/index.html

W3C's "The HTML3 Table Model"
http://www.w3.org/TR/WD-tables-951023.html

Publishing Your Web Page

"Making Web Pages Universally Accessible"
**http://www.december.com/cmc/may/1998/jan/
burg.html**

CAST's *Bobby 3.0*
http://www.cast.org/bobby/

"Web Site Garage"
http://www.websitegarage.com

"Web Development"
http://www.december.com/web/develop.html

"Suggestions for Web Pages"
http://nic.nasa.gov/nic/pages.html

GeoCities
http://www.geocities.com

Useful References

Burgstahler, Sheryl. "Making Web Pages Universally Accessible." *CMC Magazine* 5.1 (1998). http://www.december.com/cmc/mag/1998/jan/burg.html (21 Oct. 1998).

Library of Congress. "African American Odyssey." Rev. 14 Sep. 1998. http://memory.loc.gov/ammem/aaohtml/exhibit/aointro.html (21 Oct. 1998).

Lynch, Patrick J., and Sarah Horton. "Yale C/AIM Web Style Guide." Yale Center for Advanced Instructional Media. 1997. http://info.med.yale.edu/caim/manual/ (21 Oct. 1998).

Modern Language Association Committee on Computers and Emerging Technologies in Teaching and Research. "Draft Guidelines for Providing Web-Site Information." 19 July 1998. http://www.english.ohio-state.edu/People/Ulman.l/guidelines/Web_guidelines.htm (21 Oct. 1998).

P A R T 4

Documenting Electronic Sources

SECTION 4.1
Columbia Online Style

SECTION 4.2
MLA Style

SECTION 4.3
APA Style

SECTION 4.4
CMS Style

SECTION 4.5
CBE Style

In most respects this section is for reference: you've probably chosen an appropriate system of documentation by the time you arrive here, or else an instructor has made that decision for you. In the arts and humanities, the systems of the Modern Language Association (MLA) or the *Chicago Manual of Style* (CMS) are often preferred. Projects in the social sciences typically require the style of the American Psychological Association (APA); the natural sciences follow several different style manuals, though that of the Council of Biology Editors (CBE) is particularly influential.

Recently, the editors of these styles have been wrestling with the need to accommodate a growing number of electronic sources—most of them decidedly uncooperative. Over the years, printed sources have usually presented scholars with all the information they needed for documentation: authors, titles, publication information, dates, and pagination. Electronic sources haven't been so helpful. As a result, documentation systems designed for print sources have been stymied by the need to cite nontraditional items such as Web sites without authors, dates, or pages; Web sites with frames, audio clips, and streaming videos; newsgroup musings that disappear in two days; dialogues on MOOs that seem like places but aren't; and worse.

Early attempts to fit electronic sources within conventional documentation forms usually did not describe the sources adequately or help researchers to locate them. Later attempts have been more successful, but electronic items still seem like afterthoughts in most documentation systems. However, an alternative to the traditional documentation systems is offered here: Columbia Online Style (COS). COS has been written specifically to accommodate both electronic sources and conventional systems of documentation. If you are using MLA, APA, CMS, or CBE styles in a paper for conventional sources, you can select an appropriate version (COS-humanities or COS-scientific) of Columbia Online Style for all electronic materials. COS covers more types of electronic materials more consistently and elegantly than do the other major documentation systems.

However, in some instances you will be required to strictly adhere to the formats for citing electronic sources recommended by MLA, APA, CMS, or CBE style. This part of the book presents formats for citing electronic sources following each of these styles. For more information, see the style manual for the particular documentation system you are using.

Columbia Online Style

In preparing a college research project, you may use a wide variety of electronically accessed sources and services—Web sites, listservs, email, full-text databases, electronic reference books, and more. When the time comes to document these items, however, conventional citation systems may prove inadequate. Either they don't mention the types of sources you are using, or the guidelines for documenting them are cumbersome and unwieldy. That's not surprising; most citation systems were originally designed for printed documents, so they wobble as they try to accommodate sources without authors, titles, or even page numbers. Many people have attempted to address these inadequacies by compiling recommendations specifically formulated for electronic sources; however, many of these styles still fail to present a clear, logical, and comprehensive system without introducing unnecessary complexities.

An exception is the system of documentation presented in *The Columbia Guide to Online Style* (1998) by Janice R. Walker and Todd Taylor. Columbia Online Style (COS), designed expressly for electronically accessed material, acknowledges that online and computer accessed sources differ from printed ones and yet have a logic of their own that makes reliable citation possible. Unless you are specifically instructed otherwise, we recommend using the appropriate COS style to document electronic sources: COS-humanities style for projects following MLA and CMS guidelines, COS-scientific style for projects following APA and CBE guidelines. For other styles, COS guidelines can easily be adapted to conform to the specific format required.

4.1.1 COS documentation. Fortunately, you don't have to forget what you have learned about other documentation systems to use COS—it doesn't replace MLA, APA, CMS, or CBE style. Instead, COS is designed to work with all of them so that writers can document electronic sources consistently and appropriately *within* the style they are expected to use in school or at work. To use COS style, simply follow it consistently for all the electronic sources in a project, choosing the COS form best suited to the documentation style you are using for printed sources. To make this adaptation simple, COS offers forms for both major types of documentation, the author–page number form favored in humanities systems (MLA, CMS) and the author-date style preferred in the sciences (APA, CBE). In this chapter, we provide separate COS examples for humanities-style citations (Section 4.1.2) and science-style citations (Section 4.1.3)

Like the MLA and APA systems, Columbia Online Style documentation itself involves just two basic steps: inserting a note at each point where a paper or project needs documentation (Step 1) and then recording all sources used in these notes in a Works Cited or References list (Step 2).

a **(Step 1) In the body of your paper, place a note in appropriate form for every item you must document.**   For a **humanities** paper in MLA style, the in-text note will usually be an author's last name and a page number in parentheses.

    (Weinberg 38)

But most electronic sources do not have page numbers—which are, after all, a convention of printed texts. Specific references in electronic sources can be easily located using the built-in search or find features of most software packages; thus, designating the specific location of a reference within an electronic text is unnecessary. So, for electronic sources without page numbers or other consistent divisions, simply place the author's last name in parentheses after a passage that requires documentation.

    Jim Lehrer may be America's most trusted
    newsperson, its new Walter Cronkite
    (Shafer).

If an electronically accessed source has no conventional author or other person responsible for the information—a common occurrence—identify the source by the title (or by a brief description of the file when no title is given, such as for a graphics file). If the title is very long, you may use a shortened version of it.

> *USA Today* was among those to
> editorialize against the tobacco
> industry's continuing influence on
> Congress ("Tobacco").

When you cite a source without page numbers multiple times, repeat the author's name (or the short title, if there is no author) for each citation. But try to keep intrusions to a minimum—for example, by using a single note at the end of a paragraph when one source is cited throughout it. You can eliminate a parenthetical note by naming the author or title of a source in the body of the text.

> Shafer claims in a *Slate* column that
> PBS's Jim Lehrer is the new Walter
> Cronkite, America's most trusted
> newsperson.

> In "Tobacco Wields Its Clout," *USA Today*
> editorializes against the tobacco
> industry's continuing influence on
> Congress.

When citing a message from email, listservs, or other electronic forums such as MOO or chat room discussions, you may have to cite an author's alias or nickname.

> In a recent posting to the newsgroup
> alt.sport.paintball, jireem argued . . .

Note that electronic addresses are not enclosed in parentheses or angle brackets in COS style.

For **scientific** papers, the in-text note will include an author's last name followed by a date of "publication" in parentheses. For most types of publications, give only the year even if the source furnishes day and date.

```
Jim Lehrer may be America's most trusted
newsperson, its new Walter Cronkite
(Shafer, 1996).
```

You can also simply name the author in the body of your text, following the name with year of publication in parentheses.

```
Shafer (1996) claims in a Slate column
that PBS's Jim Lehrer is the new Walter
Cronkite, America's most trusted
newsperson.
```

Some electronic sources such as pages on the World Wide Web may not have dates of publication or any dates at all. In such cases for science-style references, record the date you accessed the source, giving day, month, and year.

```
Slipstream (21 May 1997) argues that the
research design is flawed, but
ksmith (22 May 1997) rejects that claim.
```

As a general rule, make all parenthetical notes as brief and inconspicuous as possible. Remember that the point of a note is to identify a source of information, not to distract readers.

For a humanities paper using Chicago Manual of Style (CMS) footnotes or endnotes, the note consists of a raised number in the text keyed to a full note either at the bottom of the page or in a separate "Notes" list at the end.

```
     20. Paul Skowronek, "Left and Right
for Rights," Trincoll Journal, 13 March
```

```
1997. http://www.trincoll.edu/~tj/
tj03.13.97/articles/comm2.htm1
(23 July 1997).
```

The COS form for CMS notes can be adapted from the
COS Humanities Form Directory in Section 4.1.2b.
You will need to study both COS forms in that section
and the CMS footnote forms in Section 4.4.

b **(Step 2) On a separate page at the end of
your paper, list every source you cited in a parenthetical note.**   This alphabetical list of sources is
usually titled "Works Cited" in humanities projects and
"References" in scientific projects. You must have a
Works Cited/References list for MLA and APA projects; in Chicago style, such a list is optional because
the notes themselves include all essential bibliographical information.

Like citations in other systems, COS items are as-
sembled from a few basic components.

• **Author.** In humanities styles, list the full name of
the author, last name first, followed by any additional authors listed in the usual order.

```
Walker, Janice R., and Todd Taylor.
```

In scientific styles, list the author's last name and
initials, followed by any additional authors.

```
Walker, J. R., & Taylor, T.
```

Many electronic sources do not have authors in the
conventional sense. A Web site, for example, may be
a collaborative effort or represent an entire institution or a corporation; even for many singly authored
electronic sources, the author's name may be missing
or may be an alias or nickname. List an "author"
when you can clearly identify someone as responsible
for a source, text, or message. List an alias if you
don't know the actual name of the person. For example, the author of an email message from cerulean
@mail.utexas.edu would be cerulean. Do not include
the author's email address.

    cerulean. "Re: Bono Rocks." Personal
        email (25 Jul. 1997).

Note that COS style does not hyphenate the word
email. When no author can be identified, list the
source on a Works Cited/References page by its title.

- **Title.** Depending on whether you are adapting COS
  to MLA or APA documentation styles, titles of electronic works might be italicized, placed between
  quotation marks, or left without any special marking.
  But titles in COS citations are never underlined because in many computer environments, underlining
  is used for hypertext links.

- **Editor, translator, or compiler.** Include the name of
  the editor, translator, or compiler, if not listed ear-
  lier. In humanities styles, precede the name with the
  appropriate abbreviations (*Ed.*, *Trans.*, or *Comp.*)
  immediately followed by the full name. In scientific
  styles, the abbreviation is enclosed in parentheses
  and follows the name.

- **Print or previous publication information.** Many
  works online are based on printed sources with conventional publication histories, and this information
  should be included in a citation just before the electronic publication information. But for other online
  sources, the electronic address or pathway is the essential publication information. Specifying a "publication medium" (*CD-ROM*, *Internet*, *online*, *WWW*)
  for an electronic source is usually unnecessary since
  the information is evident in the electronic address
  and the same information may be available in more
  than one medium. Follow the print information, if
  applicable, with the online publication information
  (see below).

- **Date of publication and/or access.** While print publications are routinely dated and archived, these
  conventions don't always suit electronic sources,
  which allow for more frequent revisions or may be
  moved or even deleted without notice. When an online or electronic source is based on a printed source

or appears in a dated format (such as the online version of a newspaper or magazine), give the original publication date of the material. For Web sites, check the home page or the source code for information about original dates of posting and updates.

For most electronic sources, provide a date of access—the day, month, and year you actually examined the material, enclosed in parentheses and following the electronic address. This date is important for establishing the version of the material you looked at in an environment that might be changing rapidly. When the date of publication of a source is the same as the date of your access to it (as it might be when you're reading an online news source or listserv message), you need to give only the date of access.

- **Electronic address.** In citations of online items, the information most important to a researcher may be the pathway or electronic address, the means by which a given source can be located. For many sources in undergraduate research projects, that electronic address is likely to be a World Wide Web uniform resource locator (URL), that is, the familiar Web address beginning http://www. URLs must be copied accurately so researchers can locate the material you are documenting. To ensure accuracy, you can usually cut and paste an address directly from a Web browser into your project.

Unfortunately, some URLs are quite long and will produce odd line breaks. Don't, however, introduce a space into a URL just to fill an awkward gap in your citation. That empty space will ruin the citation for researchers who might copy and paste it directly from your document to their Web browsers. Let the word wrap capability of your word processor break the URL (but turn off the auto hyphenation feature).

Holmes, Steven. "Black English Debate."
The New York Times 30 Dec. 1996.
http://search.nytimes.com/search/

```
daily/bin/fastweb?getdoc+site+site+
8836+4+wAAA+%28suspension%29%26OR%
26%28bridges%29%26OR%26%28%29
(28 July 1997).
```

Sometimes you can avoid long and unwieldy URLs by pointing to the main URL for a given site and then listing the links or search terms you followed to access the particular site or document. For example, the *New York Times* article shown below can be located through the newspaper's searchable index. Go directly to the search URL (http://search.nytimes .com/search/daily/) and type in the search terms "Black English Debate" to find the article.

```
Holmes, Steven. "Black English Debate:
     No Standard Assumptions." New York
     Times 30 Dec. 1996. http://search
     .nytimes.com/search/daily/ Black
     English Debate (22 Feb. 1998).
```

Note that a single blank space separates the URL from the search terms.

Some newer versions of word processors incorporate features that automatically reformat URLs and email addresses in a text document. In documents being read on a computer with Internet access, each address becomes a link that automatically opens a browser or email client and connects to the designated URL. In documents being printed, the font size and/or color may be changed, and the address is usually underlined automatically to designate a hypertext link.

http://www.awlonline.com/englishpages

When you include this URL within a citation, the word processor automatically reformats it for you.

```
Jordan-Henley, Jennifer. "Basic Skills
     Simulated Search Activity." The
```

English Pages. Addison Wesley
Longman. http://www.awlonline.com/
englishpages Basic Skills/Activity
Center (22 Sep. 1998).

Unless you are using a color printer, the colored text will appear slightly lighter than the surrounding text. Columbia Online Style recognizes that hypertext is becoming a feature of both print *and* online sources; thus, if your word processor reformats an electronic address and automatically creates a hypertext link, you should not attempt to change it. However, do not attempt to emulate it on your own either— merely underlining an electronic address in a word-processed document will not create a hypertext link in your file.

COS style also suggests that, for works to be published on the WWW, citation entries be listed using the hypertext unordered list feature rather than trying to force hanging indents. For traditional print projects, however, COS follows the hanging indent of other styles: the first line of each bibliographic entry is flush with the left-hand margin, and subsequent lines are indented one-half inch or five spaces.

COS style does not surround electronic addresses with angle brackets < >. This additional and potentially confusing punctuation is not necessary to separate an electronic address from other elements in an entry. Moreover, these characters could cause problems if you copy and paste them into a word-processed document or a hypertext composition.

A typical **Columbia Online Style Works Cited entry for an MLA-style paper in the humanities** includes the following basic information.

- Author, last name first, followed by a period and one space.
- Title of the work, followed by a period and one space. Book titles are italicized; article titles appear between quotation marks.

- Publication information (if any), followed by a period and one space. This will ordinarily include a date of publication if different from the date of access. List previous publication information (including print publication information), if known, followed by electronic publication information.

- The electronic address and any path or directory information, followed by a space. No period follows the electronic address.

- The date you accessed the information, in parentheses, followed by a period.

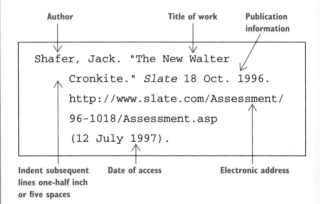

Shafer, Jack. "The New Walter
    Cronkite." *Slate* 18 Oct. 1996.
    http://www.slate.com/Assessment/
    96-1018/Assessment.asp
    (12 July 1997).

Author · Title of work · Publication information · Indent subsequent lines one-half inch or five spaces · Date of access · Electronic address

A typical **Columbia Online Style Works Cited entry for a CMS-style paper in the humanities** includes the following basic information.

- Author(s), last name first, followed by a period and one space.

- Title of the work, followed by a period (or other final punctuation mark) and enclosed between quotation marks.

- Publication information, followed by a period. This will ordinarily include a date of publication if different from the date of access. List previous publication information (including print publication information), if known, followed by information on the electronic publication.

- The electronic address, and any path or directory information, followed by a space. No period follows the electronic address.
- The date you accessed the information, in parentheses, followed by a period.

Authors   **Title**   **Publication information**

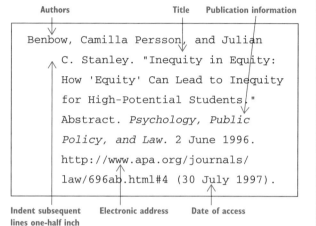

Benbow, Camilla Persson, and Julian
    C. Stanley. "Inequity in Equity:
    How 'Equity' Can Lead to Inequity
    for High-Potential Students."
    Abstract. *Psychology, Public
    Policy, and Law.* 2 June 1996.
    http://www.apa.org/journals/
    law/696ab.html#4 (30 July 1997).

Indent subsequent   **Electronic address**   **Date of access**
lines one-half inch

A typical **Columbia Online Style "References" entry for an APA-style paper in the sciences** includes the following basic information.

- Author(s), last name first, followed by a period and one space.
- Date of publication in parentheses, followed by a period and one space. Give the year first, followed by the month (do not abbreviate it), followed by the day for periodical publications; give only the year of publication for other works. If no publication date is available, use the date of access in day-month-year format.
- Title of the work, followed by a period and one space.
- Publication information (if any), followed by a period and one space. List previous publication information (including print publication information), if known, followed by information on the electronic publication.

- The electronic address and any path or directory information, followed by a space. No period follows the electronic address.

- The date you accessed the information, in parentheses, followed by a period.

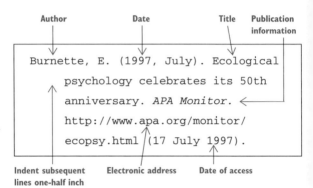

| Author | Date | Title | Publication information |

Burnette, E. (1997, July). Ecological
    psychology celebrates its 50th
    anniversary. *APA Monitor.*
    http://www.apa.org/monitor/
    ecopsy.html (17 July 1997).

Indent subsequent lines one-half inch   Electronic address   Date of access

There are so many variations to these general entries, however, that you will want to check the COS Form Directories that follow in Section 4.1.2 (Humanities) and 4.1.3 (Sciences) for the correct format of any particular entry.

4.1.2 **COS form directory—humanities (MLA).** Below you will find the COS humanities-style forms for a variety of electronic sources. Use these forms when you are writing a paper in which you use an author–page number citation system (such as MLA) for nonelectronic sources. Note that the items in this section adhere to MLA style for the names of authors and the titles of works but follow COS guidelines for the electronic portion of the citation.

To find the form you need, simply look in the Format Index for the type of source you need to document and then locate that item by number in the COS Form Directory itself. To handle more complex electronic sources and to learn more about developing standards for online style, consult *The Columbia Guide to Online Style* by Janice R. Walker and Todd Taylor (New York: Columbia UP, 1998) or its regularly updated online version at http://www.columbia.edu/cu/cup/cgos/.

COS Format Index—HUMANITIES (MLA)

4.1.2.1   Web Site—COS/Humanities (MLA)   The title of a particular Web page appears in quotation marks, and the title of the entire site is italicized.

Works Cited

Britton, Fraser. "Fraser's Page."

   Fraser's Downhill Domain. 1999.

   http://www.geocities.com/Colosseum/

   3681/index.html (9 Feb. 1999).

4.1.2.2   Web Site, Revised or Modified—COS/ Humanities (MLA)   You may specify a date that a page or site was revised or updated if such a date is given. Your date of access follows the electronic address.

Works Cited

Stasi, Mafalda. "Another Deadline,

   Another Miracle!" *La Pagina Casa Di*

   Mafalda. Rev. Mar. 1997. http://

   www.cwrl.utexas.edu/~mafi/present/

   (5 May 1997).

4.1.2.3   Web Site with a Group or Institutional Author—COS/Humanities (MLA)

Works Cited

Texas Department of Transportation. "Big

   Bend Ranch State Park: General

   Information." *TourTex 2000.* Rev. 13

```
June 1996. http://www.dot.state.tx
.us/travel/tourtex/bigbend/trv0001
.htm (5 Dec. 1996).
```

**4.1.2.4 Web Site, No Author or Institution—
COS/Humanities (MLA)** When no author or institution can be assigned to a site, begin the entry with the title of the page or the site. In the example, the title is italicized because it identifies an entire Web site.

Works Cited

The British Monarchy: The Official Web
        Site. Rev. 20 June 1997. http://
        www.royal.gov.uk/ (5 July 1997).

**4.1.2.5 Web Site Maintained by an Individual—
COS/Humanities (MLA)** A maintained site is one that usually contains links, routinely updated, to materials not created by the author(s) of the site. The site can be listed either by the person(s) maintaining it or by its name, depending on which emphasis suits your project.

Works Cited

Clark, Stephen, et al., maint.
        "Philosophy at Large." University
        of Liverpool Department of
        Philosophy. http://www.liv.ac.uk/
        ~srlclark/philos.html (15 June
        1997).

"Philosophy at Large." Maint. Stephen
        Clark, et al. University of
        Liverpool Department of Philosophy.
        http://www.liv.ac.uk/~srlclark/
        philos.html (15 June 1997).

4.1.2.6 Web Site—Government—COS/Humanities (MLA) In this example, no date is given for this frequently updated Web site because it is the same as the date of access.

Works Cited

United States Congress. "Floor Activity
in Congress This Week." *Thomas:
Legislative Information on the
Internet.* http://thomas.loc.gov/
home/hot-week.html (9 Feb. 1999).

4.1.2.7 Web Site—Corporate—COS/Humanities (MLA) The corporation or institution should be listed as the author.

Works Cited

Cedar Point, Inc. "The World's Greatest
Collection of Roller Coasters."
1997. http://www.cedarpoint.com/
coast.asp (30 June 1997).

4.1.2.8 Web Site—Book, Printed, Available On-line—COS/Humanities (MLA) Give the name of the author, the title of the work, and the publication information for the printed version if known. Then provide the title of the electronic version, if different from the original title, and the electronic publication information.

Works Cited

Austen, Jane. *Pride and Prejudice.* 1813.
Pride and Prejudice Hypertext. Ed.
H. Churchyard. 1994. http://
www.pemberley.com/janeinfo/
prideprej.html (29 July 1997).

4.1.2.9 Web Site—Book, Electronic—COS/Humanities (MLA) Provide an author, title, and date of publication. In this example, the publication of the book is sponsored by an organization listed after the title.

Works Cited

Baker, Catherine. *Your Genes, Your*
      Choices: Exploring the Issues
      Raised by Genetic Research.
      American Association for the
      Advancement of Science. 1997.
      http://www.nextwave.org/ehr/books/
      index.html (9 Feb. 1999).

4.1.2.10 Web Site—Online Article—COS/Humanities (MLA)   The title of the article in quotation marks is followed by the italicized title of the journal in which it appears. The volume number of the periodical is given, followed by a period and an issue number (if available) and date of publication.

Works Cited

University of Texas at Austin
      Undergraduate Writing Center. "Miss
      Grammars Attacks Sexist Language."
      The Writer's Block. 3.2 (1995).
      http://uwc-server.fac.utexas.edu/
      wblock/dec95.html#TOC (28 July
      1997).

4.1.2.11 Web Site—Article from a News Service or Online Newspaper—COS/Humanities (MLA)   If no author's name is given, list the name of the news source (such as Reuters or Associated Press), followed by the title of the article, the name of the news service or online newspaper, the date of the article if different from the date accessed, the electronic address, and the date accessed.

Works Cited

Associated Press. "Pathfinder's Battery
      Power Dwindles." *CNN Interactive.*
      http://www.cnn.com/TECH/9707/29/

```
pathfinder.ap/index.html (29 July
1997).
```

4.1.2.12 Web Site—Article from an Archive—COS/Humanities (MLA) Provide author, title, journal, and date as you would for a printed article, followed by the name of the archive site, the electronic address, and the date of access. In the example below, "The Compost Pile" is the name *Slate* gives to its archive of previously published articles.

```
              Works Cited
Achenbach, Joel. "The Unexamined Game
        Is Not Worth Watching." Slate 9
        May 1997. "The Compost Pile."
        http://www.slate.com/goodsport/
        97-05-09/goodsport.asp (1 June
        1997).
```

4.1.2.13 Web Site—with Frames—COS/Humanities (MLA) A Web site that uses frames may present material from other sites as well as material from within its own site. When you cannot determine the original URL of such material, list the documents by author and title and other publication information, and then give the name of the site where the source appears in a frame. Provide the electronic address of the site with frames, followed by a single blank space, and the path or links necessary to access the specific article or site (separating individual links by a forward slash). Conclude the entry with the date of access.

```
              Works Cited
Burney, Fanny. Fanny Burney and Dr.
        Johnson. London, 1842. Women of the
        Romantic Period. http://www.cwrl
        .utexas.edu/~worp/worp.html Francis
        Burney/Dr. Johnson and Fanny Burney
        (13 July 1997).
```

4.1.2.14 Web Site—Graphic or Audio File— COS/Humanities (MLA)   You may want to cite a graphic file one of two ways: either by its own URL (which you can usually find in the Netscape *Navigator* browser by selecting "Page Info" from the "View" menu) or by the Web page on which the image appears. For the graphic alone, identify the author, photographer, or artist (if known), and give its title in quotation marks or italics as appropriate, or its file name without quotation marks, followed by the date of publication (if known and if different from the date of access). Then furnish an electronic address and the date of access.

<pre>
                  Works Cited

da Vinci, Léonard. <i>La Joconde (Monna</i>

        Lisa). 1503-1506. http://www

        .culture.fr/louvre/img/photos/

        collec/peint/moyen/inv0779.jpg

        (9 Feb. 1999).
</pre>

To cite the graphic as it appears on a particular page, once again identify the artist and the title of the graphic. Then name the site on which the graphic appears, followed by any publication information and the electronic address for the page.

<pre>
da Vinci, Léonard. <i>La Joconde (Monna</i>

        Lisa). "Les Visages de la Joconde."

        By Vincent Pomorède. <i>Musée du</i>

        Louvre. http://www.culture.fr/louvre/

        francais/magazine/joconde/jocon_f.

        htm (9 Feb. 1999).
</pre>

4.1.2.15 Personal   Email—COS/Humanities (MLA)   Identify the author of the email and give the title of the message in quotation marks. Then identify the communication as "Personal email." Usually the date of the message is the same as the date you access (or read) it, so you need only give the access date in parentheses.

COS

Works Cited

```
Sherman, Lee. "Coffee Shops." Personal
     email (5 Mar. 1997).
```

4.1.2.16   Listserv—COS/Humanities   (MLA)
Identify the author of the message to a listserv. If no author's name is given, use the author's alias or email name. Then give the subject line of the message (enclosed in quotation marks) as the title, followed by the date of the message (if different from the date of access); the name of the list, in italics (if known); the address of the listserv; and the date of access.

Works Cited

```
Cook, Janice. "Re: What New Day Is
     Dawning?" 19 June 1997. Alliance
     for Computers and Writing. acw-l
     @ttacs6.ttu.edu (21 June 1997).
```

4.1.2.17   Newsgroup—COS/Humanities   (MLA)
Give the author's name (or alias), the subject line of the message as the title (enclosed in quotation marks), the date of the message (if different from the date of access), the address of the newsgroup, and the date of access.

Works Cited

```
Heady, Christy. "Buy or Lease? Depends
     on How Long You'll Keep the Car." 7
     July 1997. news:clari.biz.industry
     .automotive (14 July 1997).
```

4.1.2.18   Message from an Archive—COS/Humanities (MLA)   Identify the author; the title of the message; the date of posting; the name of the list, if known; and the address of the list. Then give the name of the archive, if available; the electronic address, followed by a single blank space; any other access information, separating individual links or commands by a forward slash; the date of access in parentheses; and the date you read the message.

Works Cited

Butler, Wayne. "Re: Techno Literacy."
6 June 1996. acw-l@ttacs6.ttu.edu.
ACW-L Archives. http://english
.ttu.edu/acw/acw-l/archive.htm
Volume II (1996)/Issue 6 (29 July
1997).

**4.1.2.19 Material from a Gopher or FTP Site—
COS/Humanities (MLA)** Give the name of the author; the title of the work; publication information if
the work appears elsewhere; the date of the document;
the protocol (*Gopher, FTP*); the electronic address, including any directory or path information; and the date
of access. If the information is accessed via the World
Wide Web, include the electronic address from the
browser.

Works Cited

Harnad, Stevan. "Minds, Machines and
Searle." *Journal of Experimental
and Theoretical Artificial
Intelligence*.1(1989).gopher://
gopher.liv.ac.uk:70/00/phil/
philos-1-files/searle.harnad
(30 July 1997).

Or the electronic address can be written to indicate the
links that lead to a particular document, separating the
links from the URL with a single blank space.

gopher://gopher.liv.ac.uk phil/
philos-1-files/searle.harnad
(30 July 1997).

**4.1.2.20 Material from a Telnet Site—COS/Hu-
manities (MLA)** Give the author of the material you
are citing (if available); the title of the material; the
date (if available); the protocol (*telnet*); the telnet ad-

dress, followed by a single blank space; any steps or commands necessary to access the site; and the date of access.

Works Cited

"Manners." *Connections*. telnet://

connections.sensemedia.net:3333

help manners (1 Mar. 1997).

4.1.2.21 Synchronous Communications (MOOs, MUDs)—COS/Humanities (APA) Identify the speaker, the type of communication and/or the title of the session, and the title of the site (if available). Then give the electronic address and date of access. In giving an address, furnish any paths, directories, or commands necessary.

Works Cited

Inept_Guest. Personal interview. *The*

Sprawl. telnet://sensemedia

.net:7777/ (21 May 1997).

4.1.2.22 Online Encyclopedia Article—COS/Humanities (MLA) Give the author of the article (if available), the title of the article, and the name of the encyclopedia. If the encyclopedia is based on a printed work, give place of publication, publisher, and date. Give any publication information about the electronic version; the service offering it (for example, *America Online*); the electronic address, including any directories and paths; and the date accessed.

Works Cited

Brown, James R. "Thought Experiments."

Stanford Encyclopedia of

Philosophy. Stanford University,

1996. http://plato.stanford

.edu/entries/thought-experiment/

thought-experiment.html (30 July

1997).

4.1.2.23 Online Dictionary/Thesaurus Entry— COS/Humanities (MLA) List the entry by the word looked up, followed by the name of the dictionary. If the dictionary is based on a printed work, give place of publication, publisher, and date. Give any publication information about the electronic version, the service offering it (for example, *America Online*), the electronic address if available, and the date accessed.

Works Cited

"Drudge." *WWWebster Dictionary.* Merriam-
        Webster, 1999. http://www.m-w.com/
        (9 Feb. 1999).

4.1.2.24 Material from a CD-ROM—COS/Humanities (MLA) Provide an author (if available), the title of the entry or article, and the name of the CD-ROM program or publication. Furnish any edition or version numbers, a series title if applicable, and available publication information.

Works Cited

Bruckheim, Allan H. "Basic First Aid."
        The Family Doctor. Vers. 3. Port-
        land: Creative Multimedia, 1993.

4.1.2.25 Material from an Online Database— COS/Humanities (MLA) Identify the author and the title of the entry or article, and give publication information for items that have appeared in print. Identify the database or information service, and furnish retrieval data and a date of access.

Works Cited

Vlasic, Bill. "In Alabama: The Soul of a
        New Mercedes?" *Business Week* 31
        Mar. 1997:70. *InfoTrac SearchBank.*
        File #A19254659 (27 July 1997).

4.1.2.26 Software—COS/Humanities (MLA) List software by its individual or corporate author. If no author is given or if the corporate author is the same as the publisher, list the software by its title. Then identify the version of the software unless the version number is part of its name (*Windows 98, Word 97*). Give place of publication (if known), publisher, and date of release.

Works Cited

The Norton Utilities. Vers. 3.2.

Cupertino, CA: Symantec, 1995.

4.1.3. **COS form directory—sciences (APA).**
Following you will find the COS science-style forms for a variety of electronic sources. Use these forms when you are writing a paper in which you use an author-date citation system (such as APA) for nonelectronic sources. Note that the items in this section adhere to APA style for the names of authors and the titles of works but follow COS guidelines for the electronic portion of the citation.

To find the form you need, simply look in the Format Index for the type of source you need to document and then locate that item by number in the COS Form Directory that follows. To handle more complex electronic sources and to learn more about developing standards for online style, consult *The Columbia Guide to Online Style* by Janice R. Walker and Todd Taylor (New York: Columbia University Press, 1998) or its regularly updated online version at http://www.columbia.edu/cu/cup/cgos/.

COS Format Index—SCIENCES (APA)

World Wide Web Citations

4.1.3.1 Web Site—COS/Sciences (APA) Capitalize the first word and any proper names in the title. The title of the site is italicized.

References

Britton, F. (1999). "Fraser's Page."
    Fraser's downhill domain. http://
    www.geocities.com/colosseum/3681/
    who.html (9 Feb. 1999).

4.1.3.2 Web Site, Revised or Modified— COS/Sciences (APA) You may specify a date that a page or site was revised or updated if such a date is given. Your date of access follows the electronic address.

References

Stasi, M. (1997, March). Another
    deadline, another miracle! *La*
    pagina casa di Mafalda (Rev. ed.).
    http://www.cwrl.utexas.edu/~mafi/
    present/ (5 May 1997).

4.1.3.3 Web Site with a Group or Institutional Author—COS/Sciences (APA)

References

Texas Department of Transportation.
    (1996, June 13). Big Bend Ranch
    State Park: General information.
    TourTex 2000 (Rev. ed.). http://
    www.dot.state.tx.us/travel/tourtex/
    bigbend/trv0001.htm (5 Dec. 1996).

4.1.3.4 Web Site, No Author or Institution— COS/Sciences (APA) When no author or institution can be assigned to a site, begin the entry with the title of the page or the site. In the example, the title is italicized because it identifies an entire Web site.

                    References

The British monarchy: The official Web
        site. (1997, June 20). (Rev. ed.).
        http://www.royal.gov.uk/ (5 July
        1997).

4.1.3.5   Web Site Maintained by an Individual—COS/Sciences (APA)   A maintained site is one that contains links, routinely updated, to materials not created by the author(s) of the site. The site can be listed either by the person(s) maintaining it or by its name, depending on which emphasis suits your project. Because this site is undated, no date follows the name of the author. In a parenthetical citation, however, give the date of access: (*Clark, 15 June 1997*).

                    References

Clark, S., et al. Philosophy at large.
        University of Liverpool Department
        of Philosophy. http://www.liv.ac
        .uk/~srlclark/philos.html (15 June
        1997).

4.1.3.6   Web Site—Government—COS/Sciences (APA)   In this example, no date is given for this frequently updated Web site because it is the same as the date of access.

                    References

U.S. Congress. Floor activity in
        Congress this week. *Thomas:*
        Legislative information on the
        Internet. http://thomas.loc
        .gov/home/hot-week.html (9 Feb.
        1999).

4.1.3.7   Web Site—Corporate—COS/Sciences (APA)   The corporation or institution should be listed as the author.

References

Cedar Point, Inc. (1997). The world's
     greatest collection of roller
     coasters. http://www.cedarpoint
     .com/coast.asp (30 June 1997).

4.1.3.8   Web Site—Book, Printed, Available On-line—COS/Sciences (APA)   Give the name of the author, the title of the work, and the publication information for the printed version if known. Then provide the title of the electronic version, if different from the original title, and the electronic publication information.

References

Austen, J. (1813). *Pride and prejudice.*
     Pride and prejudice hypertext.
     H. Churchyard (Ed.). 1994. http://
     www.pemberley.com/janeinfo/
     prideprej.html (29 July 1997).

4.1.3.9   Web Site—Book, Electronic—COS/Sciences (APA)   Provide an author, title, and date of publication. In this example, the publication of the book is sponsored by an organization listed after the title.

References

Baker, C. (1997). *Your genes, your*
     choices: Exploring the issues
     raised by genetic research.
     American Association for the
     Advancement of Science. http://
     www.nextwave.org/ehr/books/
     index.html (9 Feb. 1999).

4.1.3.10   Web Site—Online Article—COS/Sciences (APA)   In this entry, the author of the piece is an institution. Notice also that in APA style, the volume number of the periodical is italicized. Provide an issue number (if available) in parentheses after the volume number. The issue number is not italicized.

References

University of Texas at Austin
      Undergraduate Writing Center.
      (1995). Miss Grammars attacks
      sexist language. *The Writer's
      Block, 3* (2). http://uwc-server
      .fac.utexas.edu/wblock/dec95
      .html #TOC (28 July 1997).

4.1.3.11 Web Site—Article from a News Service or Online Newspaper—COS/Sciences (APA) If no author's name is given, list the name of the news source (such as Reuters or Associated Press), followed by the date of the article if different from the date accessed, the title of the article, the name of the news service or online newspaper, the electronic address, and the date accessed.

References

Associated Press. (1997, July 29).
      Pathfinder's battery power
      dwindles. *CNN Interactive.* http://
      www.cnn.com/TECH/9707/29/
      pathfinder.ap/index.html (30 July
      1997).

4.1.3.12 Web Site—Article from an Archive— COS/Sciences (APA) Provide author, title, journal, and date as you would for a printed article, followed by the name of the archive site, if applicable; the electronic address; and the date of access. In the example below, "The Compost Pile" is the name *Slate* gives to its archive of previously published articles.

References

Achenbach, J. (1997, May 9). The
      unexamined game is not worth

```
watching. Slate. The Compost Pile.
http://www.slate.com/goodsport/
97-05-09/goodsport.asp (1 June
1997).
```

4.1.3.13 Web Site—with Frames—COS/Sciences (APA)   A Web site that uses frames may present material from other sites as well as material from within its own site. When you cannot determine the original URL of such material, list the documents by author and title and other publication information, and then give the name of the site where the source appears in a frame. Provide the electronic address of the site with frames, followed by a single blank space, and the path or links necessary to access the specific article or site. Conclude the entry with the date of access.

References

```
Burney, F. (1842). Fanny Burney and Dr.
     Johnson. London. Women of the
     Romantic Period. http://www.cwrl
     .utexas.edu/~worp/worp.html Francis
     Burney/Dr. Johnson and Fanny Burney
     (13 July 1997).
```

4.1.3.14 Web Site—Graphic or Audio File—COS/Sciences (APA)   You may want to cite a graphic file one of two ways: either by its own URL (which you can usually find in the Netscape *Navigator* browser by selecting "View Document Info") or by the Web page on which the image appears. The first citation is for the photograph itself. The second citation is to the page on which the graphic appears. APA style permits a description of the source in brackets, useful in this case.

References

```
da Vinci, L. (1503-1506). La Joconde
     [Monna Lisa]. [Painting]. http://www
     .culture.fr/louvre/img/photos/
```

```
      collec/peint/moyen/inv0779.jpg
      (9 Feb. 1999).
da Vinci, L. (1503-1506). La Joconde
      [Monna Lisa]. [Painting]. In V.
      Pomarède, Les visages de la Joconde
      [Faces of the Mona Lisa]. Musée du
      Louvre. http://www.culture.fr/
      louvre/francais/magazine/joconde/
      jocon_f.htm (9 Feb. 1999).
```

Audio or video files can be treated the same way as graphics, either as separate documents or as files set in the context of particular Web pages.

4.1.3.15 Personal Email—COS/Sciences (APA) In APA style, you do not include personal email messages in the References list.

4.1.3.16 Listserv—COS/Sciences (APA) Identify the author of the message to a listserv. If no author's name is given, use the author's alias or email name. Then give the date followed by the subject line of the message as the title; the name of the list, if known, in italics; the address of the listserv; and the date of access.

```
              References
Cook, J. (1997, June 19). Re: What new
      day is dawning? Alliance for
      computers and writing. acw-1
      @ttacs6.ttu.edu (21 June 1997).
```

4.1.3.17 Newsgroup—COS/Sciences (APA) Give the author's name (or alias), the date of the posting, the subject line of the message as the title, the address of the newsgroup, and the date of access.

```
              References
Heady, C. (1997, July 7). Buy or lease?
      Depends on how long you'll keep the
```

```
car. news:clari.biz.industry
.automotive (14 July 1997).
```

4.1.3.18   Message from an Archive—COS/Sciences (APA)   Give the name of the author; the date of the message; the title of the message; the name of the listserv, if applicable; and the address of the newsgroup or listserv (if known). Next, list the title of the archive site (if available), the electronic address followed by a single blank space and any directory path or access information, and the date of access.

References

```
Butler, W. (1996, June 6). Re: Techno
     literacy. Alliance for Computers and
     Writing. acw-l@ttacs6.ttu.edu. ACW-
     L Archives. http://english.ttu.edu/
     acw/acw-l/archive.htm Volume II
     (1996)/Issue 6 (29 July 1997).
```

4.1.3.19   Material from a Gopher or FTP Site—COS/Sciences (APA)   Give the name of the author, the date; the title of the work; publication information if the work appears elsewhere; the protocol (*Gopher, FTP*); the electronic address, including any directory or path information; and the date of access. If the information is accessed via the World Wide Web, include the electronic address from the browser.

References

```
Harnad, S. (1989). Minds, machines and
     Searle. Journal of Experimental and
     Theoretical Artificial Intelligence,
     1. gopher://gopher.liv.ac.uk:70/
     00/phil/philos-1-files/searle.harnad
     (30 July 1997).
```

Or the electronic address can be written to indicate the links that lead to a particular document, separating the electronic address from the directory or path information by a single blank space.

```
gopher://gopher.liv.ac.uk phil/
    philos-1-files/searle.harnad
    (30 July 1997).
```

4.1.3.20   Material from a Telnet Site—COS/Sciences (APA)   Give the author of the material you are citing (if available); the date (if available); the title of the material; the protocol (*telnet*); the telnet address, including any steps or commands necessary to access the site; and the date of access.

References

```
Manners. Connections. telnet://
    connections.sensemedia.net:3333
    help manners (1 Mar. 1997).
```

4.1.3.21   Synchronous Communications (MOOs, MUDs)—COS/Sciences (APA)   Identify the speaker, the type of communication and/or the title of the session, and the title of the site (if available). Then give the electronic address and date of access. In giving an address, furnish any paths, directories, or commands necessary. Note that personal communications are not usually listed in the References list in APA style. However, they must be noted within the body of the paper (see p. 134).

References

```
Inept Guest. Personal interview. The
    sprawl. telnet://sensemedia
    .net:7777/ (21 May 1997).
```

4.1.3.22   Online Encyclopedia Article—COS/Sciences (APA)   Give the author of the article (if available), the date of the edition, the title of the article, and the name of the encyclopedia. If the encyclopedia is based on a printed work, identify the place of publication and the publisher. Give any publication information about the electronic version; the service offering it (for example, *America Online*); the electronic address, including any directories and paths; and the date accessed.

References

```
Brown, J. R. (1996). Thought
     experiments. Stanford encyclopedia
     of philosophy. Stanford University.
     http://plato.stanford.edu/entries/
     thought-experiment/thought-
     experiment.html (30 July 1997).
```

4.1.3.23 Online Dictionary/Thesaurus Entry—COS/Sciences (APA) List the entry by the word looked up, followed by the date of publication and the name of the dictionary. If the dictionary is based on a printed work, give the place of publication and the publisher. Give any publication information about the electronic version, the service offering it (for example, *America Online*), the electronic address if available, and the date accessed.

References

```
Drudge. (1999). WWWebster dictionary.
     Merriam-Webster. http://www
     .m-w.com/ (9 Feb. 1999).
```

4.1.3.24 Material from a CD-ROM—COS/Sciences (APA) Provide an author (if available), the date of publication, the title of the entry or article, and the name of the CD-ROM program or publication. Furnish any edition or version numbers, a series title if applicable, and available publication information.

References

```
Bruckheim, A. H. (1993). Basic first
     aid. The family doctor (Version 3).
     Portland, OR: Creative Multimedia.
```

4.1.3.25 Material from an Online Database—COS/Sciences (APA) Identify the author, the date of publication, and the title of the entry or article, and give publication information for items that have appeared in print. Identify the database or information service, and furnish retrieval data and a date of access.

References

Vlasic, B. (1997, March 31). In Alabama: The soul of a new Mercedes? *Business Week, 70. InfoTrac SearchBank.* File #A19254659 (27 July 1997).

4.1.3.26 Software—COS/Sciences (APA) List software by its individual or corporate author. If no author is given or if the corporate author is the same as the publisher, list the software by its title. APA style does not italicize the title of software in a References list. Note also the placement of the version number in parentheses and the description of the source in brackets, both following the title.

References

The Norton utilities (Version 3.2). [Computer software]. (1995). Cupertino, CA: Symantec.

MLA Style

In many professional fields in the humanities (including both English and rhetoric and composition), writers are expected to follow the conventions of documentation and format recommended by the Modern Language Association (MLA). The basic procedures for MLA documentation for electronically accessed sources are spelled out in this section. If you encounter documentation problems not discussed here, you may want to refer to the *MLA Handbook for Writers of Research Papers*, Fifth Edition, by Joseph Gibaldi. Style updates are also available at the MLA Web site at <http://www.mla.org/main mla-nf.htm>.

4.2.1 **MLA documentation.** MLA documentation involves just two basic steps: inserting an in-text note at each point that a paper or project needs documentation (Step 1) and then recording all sources used in these notes in a Works Cited list (Step 2).

a **Citing electronic sources in the humanities.** MLA guidelines do not currently include forms for many electronic sources and environments, and there is considerable debate over the forms they do present. When citing electronic sources, you can use MLA format (see pp. 177–182) or you may instead want to use the documentation style recommended by the *Columbia Guide to Online Style*; it was developed explicitly for electronic environments. Columbia Online Style (COS) for humanities papers is described on pages 133 through 156. Consult your instructor about using Columbia style for electronic and computerized sources.

Note an important difference between MLA and Columbia Online Style (COS) styles: for college papers, MLA continues to recommend (at an instructor's discretion) that the titles of books and other major works be underscored rather than italicized. COS requires italics for all such titles to avoid confusion between underscored text and hypertext links. MLA's use of angle brackets < > to surround electronic addresses can also cause problems in some applications. You may need to change the default settings in your word processor to deal with these or to use special characters in HTML files (see Section 3.4). COS style, of course, avoids these problems. But do not mix the two formats; consistency in citation formats is important if the elements are to be easily understood by readers. COS-humanities style is designed to *replace* MLA style for citation of electronic sources and to work *with* MLA forms for citing conventional print sources.

b **(Step 1) In the body of your paper, place a note in parentheses to identify the source of each passage or idea you must document.** Such a note ordinarily consists of an author's last name and a page number—or a paragraph number for the few electronic sources that have them. For example, here is a sentence that includes a direct quotation from *Ralph Bunche: An American Life* by Brian Urquhart.

```
Ralph Bunche never wavered in his belief
that the races in America had to learn
to live together: "In all of his
experience of racial discrimination
Bunche never allowed himself to become
bitter or to feel racial hatred"
(Urquhart 435).
```

The author's name and the page number of the source are separated by a single typed space.

In MLA documentation, page numbers are not preceded by *p.* or *pp.* or by a comma.

```
(Urquhart 435)
(Bly 253-54)
```

You can shorten a note by naming the author of the source in the body of the essay; then the note consists only of a page number. This is a common and readable form, one you should use regularly.

```
Brian Urquhart, a biographer of Ralph
Bunche, asserts that "in all of his
experience of racial discrimination
Bunche never allowed himself to become
bitter or to feel racial hatred" (435).
```

As a general rule, make all parenthetical notes as brief and inconspicuous as possible. Remember that the point of a note is to identify a source of information, not to distract or impress readers.

The parenthetical note is usually placed after a passage needing documentation, typically at the end of a sentence and inside the final punctuation mark. However, with a quotation long enough (more than four typed lines) to require indention, the parenthetical note falls outside the final punctuation mark. Compare the following examples.

SHORT QUOTATION (NOT INDENTED)

```
Ralph Bunche never wavered in his belief
that the races in America had to learn
to live together: "In all of his
experience of racial discrimination
Bunche never allowed himself to become
bitter or to feel racial hatred"
(Urquhart 435). He continued to
work . . .
```

The note is placed inside the final punctuation mark.

LONG QUOTATION (INDENTED TEN SPACES)

```
Winner of the Nobel Peace Prize in 1950,
Ralph Bunche, who died in 1971, left an
enduring legacy:

          His memory lives on, especially
          in the long struggle for human
          dignity and against racial
          discrimination and bigotry, and
          in the growing effectiveness of
          the United Nations in resolving
          conflicts and keeping the
          peace. (Urquhart 458)
```

The note is placed outside the final punctuation mark.

Following are guidelines to use when preparing in-text notes.

1. When two or more sources are cited within a single sentence, the parenthetical notes appear right after the statements they support.

```
While the budget cuts might go deeper
than originally reported (Kinsley 42),
there is no reason to believe that
"throwing more taxpayers' dollars into a
bottomless pit" (Doggett 62) will do
much to reform "one of the least
productive job training programs ever
devised by the federal government"
(Will 28).
```

Notice that a parenthetical note is always placed outside any quotation marks but before the period that ends the sentence.

2. When you cite more than one work by a single author in a paper, a parenthetical note listing only the author's last name could refer to more than one book or article on the Works Cited page. To avoid confusion, place a comma after the author's name and identify the particular work being cited, using a shortened title. For example, a Works Cited page might list the following four works by Richard D. Altick.

```
                Works Cited
Altick, Richard D. The Art of Literary
        Research. New York: Norton, 1963.
---. The Shows of London. Cambridge:
        Belknap-Harvard, 1978.
---. Victorian People and Ideas. New
        York: Norton, 1973.
---. Victorian Studies in Scarlet. New
        York: Norton, 1977.
```

The first time—and every subsequent time—you refer to a work by Richard Altick, you need to identify it by a shortened title in the parenthetical note.

```
(Altick, Shows 345)
(Altick, Victorian People 190-202)
(Altick, Victorian Studies 59)
```

3. When you need to document a work without an author—an unsigned article in a magazine or newspaper, for example—simply list the title, shortened if necessary, and the page number.

```
("In the Thicket" 18)
("Students Rally" A6)
```

```
                Works Cited
"In the Thicket of Things." Texas
      Monthly Apr. 1994: 18.
"Students Rally for Academic Freedom."
      The Chronicle of Higher Education
      28 Sept. 1994: A6.
```

4. When you need to cite more than a single work in one note, separate the citations with a semicolon.

```
(Polukord 13-16; Ryan and Weber 126)
```

5. When a parenthetical note would be awkward, refer to the source in the body of the essay itself.

```
In "Hamlet's Encounter with the
Pirates," Wentersdorf argues . . .

Under "Northwest Passage" in Collier's
Encyclopedia . . .

The Arkansas State Highway Map
indicates . . .
```

```
Software such as Microsoft's

FoxPro . . .
```

Occasions when parenthetical notes might be awkward include the following.

- When you wish to refer to an entire article, not just to a passage or several pages
- When the author is a group or institution—for example, the editors of *Time* or the Smithsonian Institution
- When the citation is to a personal interview or an unpublished speech or letter
- When the item doesn't have page numbers—for example, a map, a cartoon, a work of art, a videotape, or a play in performance
- When the item is a reference work arranged alphabetically
- When the item is a government document with a name too long for a convenient in-text note
- When the item is computer software or an electronic source without conventional page numbers (see also pp. 134–137 for more on using parenthetical notes with electronic sources)

Individual entries in the MLA Form Directory (Section 4.2.2) indicate when to avoid an in-text parenthetical note.

c **(Step 2) On a separate page at the end of your paper, list every source cited in a parenthetical note.** This alphabetical list of sources is titled "Works Cited." The Works Cited entry for Brian Urquhart's biography of Bunche discussed on pages 169 and 170 would look like this.

```
Werstine, Paul. "Hypertext and Editorial

     Myth." Early Modern Literary

     Studies 3.3 (1998): 19 pars. 18

     Apr. 1998 <http://www.humanities
```

```
.ualberta.ca/emls/03-3/wersshak
.html>.
```

The first few entries on a full Works Cited page might look like this.

Subsequent lines indented   "Works Cited"   All items
one-half inch or five spaces   centered   double spaced

```
            Works Cited
"Bataan Death March." Encyclopaedia
    Britannica: Micropedia. 1985 ed.
Berger, Joseph. "Once Rarely Explored,
    the Holocaust Gains Momentum as a
    School Subject." The New York
    Times 3 October 1988, sec. A: 16.
Hoyt, Edwin P. Japan's War. New York:
    McGraw, 1986.
Werstine, Paul. "Hypertext and
    Editorial Myth." Early Modern
    Literary Studies 3.3 (1998): 19
    pars. 18 Apr. 1998 <http://www
    .humanities.ualberta.ca/emls/
    03-3/wersshak.html>.
```

A typical **MLA Works Cited entry for an electronic source** may include the following information, though few will require all the elements. (See also COS-humanities style in Section 4.1.2.)

- Author, last name first, followed by a period and one space.

- Title of the work, followed by a period and one space. Book titles are underlined; article titles appear between quotation marks.

- Print publication information (if any), followed by a period and one space.

- Title of the electronic site, underlined, followed by a period and one space.

- Editor (if any) of the electronic site, database, or text, with role indicated (for example, *Ed.*), followed by a period and a space.

- Version or volume number (if any) of the source, usually followed by a period.

- Date of electronic publication or most recent update, followed by a period.

- Identity of institution or group (if any) sponsoring the electronic site, followed by a period and a space.

- The date you accessed the information, followed by a space.

- The electronic address between angle brackets < >, followed by a period.

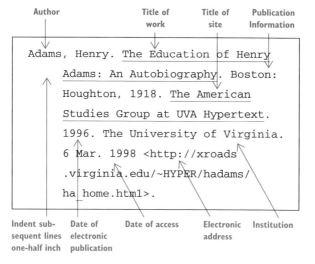

Author   Title of   Title of   Publication
                work   site   Information

    Adams, Henry. The Education of Henry
        Adams: An Autobiography. Boston:
        Houghton, 1918. The American
        Studies Group at UVA Hypertext.
        1996. The University of Virginia.
        6 Mar. 1998 <http://xroads
        .virginia.edu/~HYPER/hadams/
        ha home.htm1>.

Indent sub-   Date of   Date of access   Electronic   Institution
sequent lines   electronic   address
one-half inch   publication

There are so many variations to these general entries, however, that you will want to check the MLA Form Directory that follows in Section 4.2.2 for the correct format of any unusual entry.

The Works Cited page itself follows the body of the essay (and endnotes, if there are any). It lists bibliographical information on all the materials you used in composing an essay. You do not, however, include sources you examined but did not cite in the body of the paper itself.

When an author has more than one work on the Works Cited list, those works are listed alphabetically under the author's name using this form.

```
Altick, Richard D. The Shows of London.
     Cambridge: Belknap-Harvard, 1978.
---. Victorian People and Ideas. New
     York: Norton, 1973.
---. Victorian Studies in Scarlet. New
     York: Norton, 1977.
```

Works published since 1900 include a publisher's name. Publishers' names should be shortened whenever possible. Drop words such as *Company*, *Inc.*, *LTD*, *Bro.*, and *Books*. Abbreviate *University* to *U* and *University Press* to *UP*. When possible, shorten a publisher's name to one word. Here are some suggested abbreviations.

Barnes and Noble Books	Barnes
Doubleday and Co., Inc.	Doubleday
Harvard University Press	Harvard UP
University of Chicago Press	U of Chicago P
The Viking Press	Viking

4.2.2. MLA form drectory. Below you will find the MLA Works Cited and parenthetical note forms for selected electronic sources. Simply locate the type of source you need to cite in the Format Index and then locate that item by number in the list that follows. MLA provides only a limited number of types of electronic sources and examples. You will need to review the elements above to determine how to cite other types of electronic sources. You may want to consider using the Columbia Online Style (COS) humanities format instead of MLA style for citation of electronic sources in a paper that uses MLA style for citation of print sources. (For more information, see 4.1.)

MLA Format Index

4.2.2.1 Computer Software—MLA   Give the author if known, the software title, the version number if any (for example: Microsoft <u>Word</u>. Vers. 7.0), the manufacturer, the date, and (optionally) the system needed to run it. Name the software in your text rather than use an in-text note. For example, you could begin a sentence with something like this: "With software such as Microsoft's <u>FoxPro</u>. . . ."

```
                   Works Cited
FoxPro. Vers. 2.5. Redmond: Microsoft,
       1993.
```

4.2.2.2. WWW Page—Generic—MLA   The variety of Web pages is staggering, so you will have to adapt your documentation to particular sources. In general, provide author; title of the work; print publication information (if any); title of the electronic site, underlined; editor, with role appropriately indicated (for example, *Ed.*); version or volume number (if any) of the source; date of electronic publication or most recent update; identity of the institution or group (if any) sponsoring the electronic site; date you accessed the information; and electronic address between angle brackets < >. Since most Web sites do not have page numbers, avoid in-text parenthetical citations by identifying the site in your paper itself. A citation for a particular page within a site might look like the following.

Works Cited

"Hubble Catches Up to a Blue Straggler
    Star." <u>Space Telescope Science
    Institute</u>. 29 Oct. 1997. NASA. 28
    Nov. 1997 <http://oposite
    .stsci.edu/pubinfo/PR/97/35/>.

A citation of the entire site might be somewhat different.

Works Cited

<u>Space Telescope Science Institute Home
    Page</u>. 20 Nov. 1997. NASA. 28 Nov.
    1997 <http://www.stsci.edu/>.

4.2.2.3 WWW—Online Book—MLA Since most online books do not have page numbers, avoid in-text parenthetical citations by identifying the site in your paper itself. Give both an original date of publication of the electronic source and the date you accessed the information.

Works Cited

Dickens, Charles. <u>A Christmas Carol</u>.
    London, 1843. <u>The Electronic Text
    Center</u>. Ed. David Seaman. Dec.
    1997. U of Virginia Library. 4 Feb.
    1998 <http://etext.lib.virginia
    .edu/cgibin/browse-mixed?id=
    DicChri&tag=public&images=images/
    modeng&data=/lv1/Archive/
    eng-parsed>.

**4.2.2.4 WWW—Online Scholarly Journal—
MLA** Since most online articles do not have page
numbers, avoid in-text parenthetical citations by identifying the site in your paper itself.

Works Cited

Katz, Seth, Janice Walker, and Janet
      Cross. "Tenure and Technology: New
      Values, New Guidelines." <u>Kairos</u> 2.1
      (1997). 20 July 1997 <http://
      english.ttu.edu/kairos/2.1/index_f
      .htm1>.

**4.2.2.5 WWW—Online Popular Magazine—
MLA** Since most online articles do not have page
numbers, avoid in-text parenthetical citations by identifying the site in your paper itself.

Works Cited

Shafer, Jack. "The New Walter Cronkite."
      <u>Slate</u> 18 Oct. 1996. 12 July 1997
      <http://www.slate.com/Assessment/
      96-10-18/Assessment.asp>.

**4.2.2.6 WWW—Online Newspaper Editorial—
MLA** Since most online newspaper stories or editorials do not have page numbers, avoid in-text parenthetical citations by identifying the site in your paper itself.
Here the date of the editorial and the date of access to it
are the same.

Works Cited

"The Proved and the Unproved."
      Editorial. <u>New York Times on the
      Web</u> 13 July 1997. 13 July 1997
      <http://www.nytimes.com/yr/mo/day/
      editorial/13sun1.htm1>.

4.2.2.7 WWW—Personal Home Page

Works Cited

Yumibe, Joshua. Home page. 3 Mar. 1997
        <http://www.d1a.utexas.edu/depts/
        drc/yumibe/homeward.htm1>.

4.2.2.8. Listserv/Newsgroup/Usenet Newsgroup-MLA. When citing material from a listserv, identify the author of the document or posting; put the subject line of the posting between quotation marks, followed by the date on which the item was originally posted and the words *Online posting;* give the name of the listserv, followed by the date you accessed the item, and the electronic address in angle brackets. Because there will be no page number to cite, avoid an in-text parenthetical citation by naming the author in the text of your paper, with a sentence such as "Cook argues in favor of . . . ."

Works Cited

Cook, Janice. "Re: What New Day Is
        Dawning?" 19 June 1997. Online
        posting. Alliance for Computers and
        Writing Listserv. 4 Feb 1998 <acw-1
        @ttacs6.ttu.edu>.

Heady, Christy. "Buy or Lease? Depends
        on How Long You'll Keep the Car."
        7 July 1997. Online posting.
        ClariNet. 14 July 1997 <news:clari
        .biz.industry.automotive>.

4.2.2.9. Synchronous Communication (MOOs, MUDs)—MLA Provide the speaker and/or site, the title of the session or event, the date of the session, the forum for the communication (if specified), the date of access, and the electronic address.

Works Cited

Inept_Guest. Discussion of disciplinary
        politics in rhet/comp. 12 Mar.

```
1998. LinguaMOO. 12 Mar. 1998
<telnet://lingua.utdallas.edu:8888>.
```

4.2.2.10   Email—MLA   Identifying the communication in the essay itself is preferable to a parenthetical citation. Note the hyphen in *e-mail*.

```
              Works Cited
Pacheco, Miguel. "Re: R-ball?" E-mail to
     the author. 14 Apr. 1997.
```

4.2.2.11   CD-ROM/Diskette Database or Publication—MLA   To cite a CD-ROM or similar electronic database, provide basic information about the source itself—author, title, and publication information. Identify the publication medium (*CD-ROM; Diskette; Magnetic tape*) and the name of the vendor if available. (The vendor is the company publishing or distributing the database.) Conclude with the date of electronic publication.

```
              Works Cited
Bevington, David. "Castles in the Air:
     The Morality Plays." The Theater of
     Medieval Europe: New Research in
     Early Drama. Ed. Simon Eckchard.
     Cambridge: Cambridge UP, 1993. MLA
     Bibliography. CD-ROM.
     SilverPlatter. Feb. 1995.
```

Parenthetical note: (Bevington 98)

For a CD-ROM database that is often updated (ProQuest, for example), you must provide publication dates for the item you are examining and for the data disk itself.

```
              Works Cited
Alva, Sylvia Alatore, "Differential
     Patterns of Achievement Among
     Asian-American Adolescents."
```

```
Journal of Youth and Adolescence 22
(1993): 407-23. ProQuest General
Periodicals. CD-ROM. UMI-ProQuest.
June 1994.
```

Parenthetical note: (Alva 407-10)

Cite a book, encyclopedia, play, or other item published on CD-ROM or diskette just as if it were a printed source, adding the medium of publication (*Diskette* or *CD-ROM*, for example). When page numbers aren't available, use the author's name in the text of the paper to avoid a parenthetical citation. For example, you might use a sentence that begins "Bolter argues . . . ."

Works Cited

```
Bolter, Jay David. Writing Space: A
     Hypertext. Diskette. Hillsdale:
     Erlbaum, 1990.
```

4.2.2.12 Reference Work or Encyclopedia (Online)—MLA With familiar reference works, especially those revised regularly, identify the edition you are using by its date. You may omit the names of editors and most publishing information. No page number is given in the parenthetical note when a work is arranged alphabetically. A citation for an online encyclopedia article would include a date of access and electronic address. However, the online version might not list an author.

Works Cited

```
"Northwest Passage." Britannica Online.
     Vers. 98.1. 1 Nov. 1997.
     Encyclopaedia Britannica. 30 Nov.
     1997 <http://www.eb.com:180/
     cgibin/g?DocF=micro/430/12.html>.
```

APA Style

In many social science and related courses (anthropology, education, home economics, linguistics, political science, psychology, sociology), writers are expected to follow the conventions of documentation recommended by the American Psychological Association (APA). The basic procedures for APA documentation are spelled out in this section. A full explanation of APA procedures is provided by the *Publication Manual of the American Psychological Association*, fourth edition (1994), available in most college libraries.

Citing Electronic Sources in the Social Sciences.
APA documentation offers forms for documenting some electronic sources, which we present on pages 190 through 193. For electronic items not covered by specific APA forms, you may want to use the documentation style recommended by the *Columbia Guide to On-line Style*. The citation examples in COS-scientific style were developed explicitly for electronic forms and cover more different types of sources than any other style. But do not mix the two formats; consistency in citation formats is essential if the elements of the citation are to be readily understood. COS-scientific style is designed to *replace* APA style for citation of electronic sources and work *with* APA forms for citing conventional print sources. However, when it is necessary to use APA format for citing electronically accessed and published sources, this section presents examples following the guidelines in the *Publication Manual*. Columbia Online Style (COS) for science papers is described on pages 156 through 167. Consult your instructor about using COS for electronic and computerized sources.

4.3.1   APA documentation. APA documentation involves just two basic steps: inserting an in-text note at each point where a paper or project needs documentation (Step 1) and then recording all sources used in these notes in a References list (Step 2).

a **(Step 1) In the body of your paper, place a note to identify the source of each passage or idea you must document.** In its most common form, this APA note consists of the last name of the source's author, followed immediately by the year the material was published, in parentheses. For example, here is a sentence derived from information in an article by E. Tebeaux titled "Ramus, Visual Rhetoric, and the Emergence of Page Design in Medical Writing of the English Renaissance," published in 1991.

```
According to Tebeaux (1991), technical
writing developed in important ways in
the English Renaissance.
```

Another basic form of the APA parenthetical note places the author's last name and a date between parentheses. This form is used when the author's name is not mentioned in the sentence itself. Notice that a comma follows the author's name within the parentheses.

```
Technical writing developed in important
ways during the English Renaissance
(Tebeaux, 1991).
```

A page number may be given for indirect citations and *must* be given for direct quotations. A comma follows the date if page numbers are given. Page numbers are preceded by *p.* or *pp.*

```
During the English Renaissance, writers
began to employ "various page design
strategies to enhance visual access"
(Tebeaux, 1991, p. 413).
```

When appropriate, the documentation may be distributed throughout a passage.

```
Tebeaux (1991) observes that for writers
in the late sixteenth century, the
philosophical ideas of Peter Ramus
"provided a significant impetus to major
changes in page design" (p. 413).
```

APA parenthetical notes should be as brief and inconspicuous as possible.

Following are some guidelines to use when preparing in-text notes.

1. When two or more sources are used in a single sentence, the notes are inserted as needed after the statements they support.

```
While Porter (1981) suggests that the
ecology of the aquifer might be hardier
than suspected, "given the size of the
drainage area and the nature of the
subsurface rock" (p. 62), there is no
reason to believe that the county needs
another shopping mall in an area
described as "one of the last outposts
of undisturbed nature in the state"
(Martinez, 1982, p. 28).
```

Notice that a parenthetical note is placed outside quotation marks but before the period ending the sentence.

2. When a single source provides a series of references, you need not repeat the name of the author until other sources interrupt the series. After the first reference, page numbers are sufficient until another citation intervenes. Even then, you need repeat only the author's last name, not a date, when the reference occurs within a single paragraph.

```
. . . The council vetoed zoning approval
for a mall in an area described by
```

Martinez (1982) as the last outpost of
undisturbed nature in the state. The
area provides a "unique environment for
several endangered species of birds and
plant life" (p. 31). The birds,
especially the endangered vireo, require
breeding spaces free from encroaching
development (Harrison & Cafiero, 1979).
Rare plant life is similarly endangered
(Martinez).

3. **When you cite more than one work written by an author in a single year,** assign a small letter after the date to distinguish between the author's two works.

(Rosner, 1991a)
(Rosner, 1991b)
The charge is raised by Rosner (1991a),
quickly answered by Anderson (1991), and
then raised again by Rosner (1991b).

4. **When you need to cite more than a single work in a note,** separate the citations with a semi-colon and list them in alphabetical order.

(Searle, 1993; Yamibe, 1995)

5. **When you are referring to a Web site** (though not a particular Web document), you can give the electronic address directly in the paper. The site does not need to be added to the References list, according to APA style. (See also pp. 156–167 on COS-scientific style for more on citing electronically accessed sources.)

More information about psychology as a
profession is available on the American

Psychological Association's World Wide
Web site at http://www.apa.org/.

b **(Step 2) On a separate page at the end of
your paper, list every source cited in an in-text
note.** This alphabetical list of sources is titled "References." A References page entry for an article on medical writing in the Renaissance by E. Tebeaux would look like the following if it were in a *professional* paper submitted for publication to an APA journal.

Tebeaux, E. (1991). Ramus, visual
rhetoric, and the emergence of page
design in medical writing of the English
Renaissance. Written Communication, 8,
411-445.

However, most college papers won't be typeset; in fact, APA style describes them as "final copy." (See *Publication Manual of the American Psychological Association*, 4th ed., pp. 334–36, for an explanation of this principle.) Consequently, **References list items in student essays ought to look the way such entries appear in APA journal articles themselves—with hanging indents of five spaces rather than paragraph indents.** APA also permits the titles of books and comparable works to be italicized rather than underlined. We recommend this style for book titles and other terms needing emphasis in final copies (such as student papers) when the instructor permits it. (See p. 138 for a discussion of italics versus underlining.)

Here, then, is how Tebeaux's article would appear in the References list of a *college paper* in APA "final copy" style.

Tebeaux, E. (1991). Ramus, visual
    rhetoric, and the emergence of page
    design in medical writing of the
    English Renaissance. *Written
    Communication, 8,* 411-445.

We use hanging indents for APA References entries throughout the handbook.

Subsequent lines indented one-half inch or five spaces   "References" centered   All items double spaced

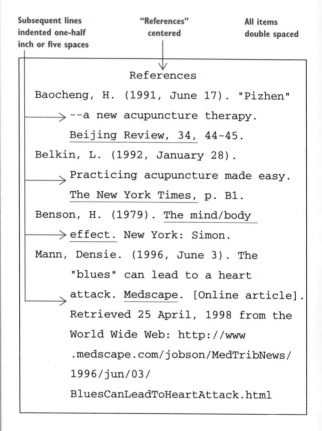

```
                  References
Baocheng, H. (1991, June 17). "Pizhen"
    --a new acupuncture therapy.
    Beijing Review, 34, 44-45.
Belkin, L. (1992, January 28).
    Practicing acupuncture made easy.
    The New York Times, p. B1.
Benson, H. (1979). The mind/body
    effect. New York: Simon.
Mann, Densie. (1996, June 3). The
    "blues" can lead to a heart
    attack. Medscape. [Online article].
    Retrieved 25 April, 1998 from the
    World Wide Web: http://www
    .medscape.com/jobson/MedTribNews/
    1996/jun/03/
    BluesCanLeadToHeartAttack.html
```

A typical **APA References entry for an online or WWW document** includes the following basic information.

- Author(s), last name first, followed by a period and one space.

- Date of publication in parentheses, followed by a period and one space. Give the year first, followed by the month (do not abbreviate it), followed by the day, if necessary.

- Title of the work, followed by a period and one space.

- Information about the form of the information—*On line, CD-ROM, Computer software*—in brackets, followed by a period and one space. Note that *on-line* is hyphenated in APA style.

- Path statement or electronic address, including the date of access. No period follows the path statement.

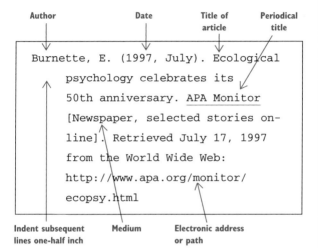

Author   Date   Title of   Periodical
                            article   title

```
Burnette, E. (1997, July). Ecological
     psychology celebrates its
     50th anniversary. APA Monitor
     [Newspaper, selected stories on-
     line]. Retrieved July 17, 1997
     from the World Wide Web:
     http://www.apa.org/monitor/
     ecopsy.html
```

Indent subsequent   Medium   Electronic address
lines one-half inch   or path

There are many variations to these generic entries, however, so you should check the *Publication Manual of the American Psychological Association* (1994) when you do a major APA-style project. For advice on writing a student paper, consult the APA manual. For the latest updates on electronic documentation, check the APA Web site at http://www.apa.org/students. APA provides only a limited number of types of electronic sources and examples. You will need to review the elements above to determine how to cite other types of sources. You may also want to review COS-scientific style in 4.1.

The References list itself appears on its own page following the body of the essay (and a footnote page if there is one). It lists bibliographical information on all the materials you used in composing an essay.

4.3.2 APA form directory. In this section, you will find the APA References page and parenthetical note forms for a variety of electronically accessed sources. Locate the type of source you need to cite in the Format Index and then locate the item by number in the list that follows. To determine how to cite other types of electronic sources, you may want to consider using the Columbia Online Style (COS) scientific format in Section 4.1 instead of APA style. Do not mix forms, however. COS-scientific style is designed to *replace* APA style for citations of electronically accessed sources and to work *with* APA style citations of print sources.

APA Format Index

Electronic Sources

4.3.2.1   Computer software

4.3.2.2   Online source

4.3.2.3   WWW page—generic

4.3.2.4   WWW page—online scholarly article

4.3.2.5   WWW page—online newspaper article

4.3.2.6   WWW page—online abstract

4.3.2.7   Email

4.3.2.1 Computer Software—APA   Do not underline or italicize the titles of software. List authors only when they own the product.

```
                  References
Adobe Photoshop 4.0 [Computer software].

     (1996). Mountain View, CA: Adobe

     Systems.
```

Parenthetical note:

```
In Adobe Photoshop (1996) . . .
```

4.3.2.2 Online Source, Archived Listserv, or Usenet Newsgroup—APA   For all online sources, provide the same information you would give for printed sources (author, date, title of article, publication information). Then identify the "medium" of the source in brackets, that is, the kind of material it is. Finally, furnish the date of access and a path statement to guide readers to the material, usually an electronic address or the protocol, directory, and file name of the source.

References

Dubrowski, J. (1994, October 18). Mixed
    signals from Washington leave
    automakers puzzled [Clarinet news
    item]. Retrieved October 20, 1995
    from C-reuters@clarinet.com
    Directory:/biz/industry/automotive

Parenthetical note:

Dubrowski (1994) reports . . .
(Dubrowski, 1994)

4.3.2.3   WWW Page—Generic—APA

References

Johnson, C. W., Jr. (1997, February 13).
    How our laws are made [Article
    posted on Web site Thomas].
    Retrieved May 27, 1997 from the
    World Wide Web: http://thomas
    .loc.gov/home/lawsmade.toc.html

Parenthetical note:

Johnson (1997) explains . . .
(Johnson, 1997)

4.3.2.4   WWW Page—Online Scholarly Article—APA   Because it is immediately obvious that the source is an article from a scholarly journal, no bracketed explanation of the medium is necessary.

References

Fine, M. A., & Kurdek, L. A. (1993).
    Reflections on determining

authorship credit and authorship
order on faculty-student
collaborations. American
Psychologist, 48, 1141-1147.
Retrieved July 17, 1997 from the
World Wide Web: http://www.apa
.org/journals/amp/kurdek.html

Parenthetical note:

Fine and Kurdek (1993) report . . .
(Fine & Kurdek, 1993)

4.3.2.5   WWW Page—Online Newspaper Article —APA

References

Cohen, E. (1997, January 17). Shrinks
aplenty online but are they
credible? The New York Times
[Newspaper, article in archives].
Retrieved May 5, 1997 from the
World Wide Web: http://search
.nytimes.com/search/daily/bin/
fastweb?getdoc+site+site+4842+4
+wAAA+%28psychology%29%26OR%26%28%
29%26OR%26%28%29

Parenthetical note:

Cohen (1997) asks . . .
(Cohen, 1997)

4.3.2.6   WWW Page—Online Abstract—APA

References

Shilkret, R., & Nigrosh, E. (1997).
Assessing students' plans for
college [Abstract]. Journal of
Counseling Psychology, 44, 222-231.

```
Retrieved July 1, 1997 from the

World Wide Web: http://www.apa.org/

journals/cou/497ab.html#10
```

Parenthetical note:

```
Shilkret and Nigrosh (1997) report . . .

(Shilkret & Nigrosh, 1997)
```

4.3.2.7. Email—APA Electronic communications not stored or archived have limited use for researchers. APA style treats such information (as well as email) like personal communication. Because personal communications are not available to other researchers, no mention is made of them in the References list. Personal communications should, however, be acknowledged in the body of the essay in parenthetical notes.

Parenthetical note:

```
According to Rice (personal

communication, October 14, 1994) . . .
```

CMS Style

Writers who prefer full footnotes or endnotes rather than in-text notes often use the "humanities style" of documentation recommended in *The Chicago Manual of Style* (14th ed., 1993). Basic procedures for this CMS documentary-note system are spelled out in the following sections. If you encounter documentation problems not discussed below or prefer the author-date style of CMS documentation, refer to the full manual or to *A Manual for Writers of Term Papers, Theses, and Dissertations* (6th ed., 1996).

A Note on Citing Electronic Sources. CMS documentation does not currently offer specific forms for many electronic sources, although several of them are covered on pages 199 through 201. When citing such items, you may want to use the documentation style recommended by the *Columbia Guide to Online Style;* it was developed explicitly for research in electronic environments. Columbia Online Style (COS) for humanities papers is described in Section 4.1. Consult your instructor about using Columbia style for electronic sources.

Because notes in CMS humanities style include full publishing information, separate bibliographies are optional in CMS-style papers. However, both notes and bibliographies are covered below in separate sections.

4.4.1   CMS notes

a   (Step 1) In the text of your paper, place a raised number after any sentence or clause you need to document.   These note numbers follow any punctuation marks, except for dashes, and run consecutively throughout a paper. For example, a direct quotation from Brian Urquhart's *Ralph Bunche: An American Life* is here followed by a raised note number.

```
Ralph Bunche never wavered in his belief
that the races in America had to learn
to live together: "In all of his
experience of racial discrimination
Bunche never allowed himself to become
bitter or to feel racial hatred."1
```

The number is keyed to the first note (see Step 2). To create such a raised, or "superscript," number, select "superscript" from your word-processing font options or, on a typewriter, roll the carriage down slightly and type the figure.

b   (Step 2) Link every note number to a footnote or endnote.   The basic CMS note itself consists of a note number, the author's name (in normal order), the title of the work, full publication information within parentheses, and appropriate page numbers. The first line of the note is indented like a paragraph.

> 1. Brian Urquhart, *Ralph Bunche: An American Life* (New York: Norton, 1993), 435.

To document particular types of electronic sources, see Section 4.4.3, the CMS Form Directory. For other types of sources, see the *Publication Manual of the American Psychological Association.*

CMS style allows you to choose whether to place your notes at the bottom of each page (footnotes) or in a single list titled "Notes" at the end of your paper (endnotes). Endnotes are more common now than footnotes and easier to manage—though some word processors can arrange footnotes at the bottom of pages automatically. Individual footnotes are single spaced, with double spaces between them. End notes are double-spaced throughout.

Following are some guidelines to use when preparing notes.

1. When two or more sources are cited within a single sentence, the note numbers appear right after the statements they support.

> While some in the humanities fear that electronic technologies may make the "notion of wisdom" obsolete,[2] others suggest that technology must be the subject of serious study even in elementary and secondary school.[3]

The notes for this sentence would appear as follows.

> 2. Sven Birkerts, *The Gutenberg Elegies: The Fate of Reading in an Electronic Age* (Boston: Faber and Faber, 1994), 139.

> 3. Neil Postman, "The Word Weavers/The World Makers," in *The End of Education: Redefining the Value of School* (New York: Alfred A. Knopf, 1995), 172-93.

Observe that note 2 documents a particular quotation while note 3 refers to a full book chapter.

2. When you cite a work several times in a project, the first note gives full information about author(s), title, and publication.

> 1. Helen Wilkinson, "It's Just a Matter of Time," *Utne Reader* (May/June 1995): 66-67.

Then, in shorter projects, any subsequent citations require only the last name of the author(s) and page number(s).

> 3. Wilkinson, 66.

In longer projects, the entry may also include a shortened title to make references from page to page clearer.

> 3. Wilkinson, "Matter of Time," 66.

If you cite the same work again immediately after a full note, you may use the Latin abbreviation *Ibid.* (meaning "in the same place"), followed by the page number(s) of the citation.

> 4. Newt Gingrich, "America and the Third Wave Information Age," in *To Renew America* (New York, HarperCollins, 1995), 51.
>
> 5. Ibid., 55.

To avoid using *Ibid.* when documenting the same source in succession, simply use a page reference—for example, (*55*)—within the text itself. When successive citations are to exactly the same page, *Ibid.* alone can be used.

> 4. Newt Gingrich, "America and the Third Wave Information Age," in *To Renew America* (New York, HarperCollins, 1995), 51.
>
> 5. Ibid.

Here's how a set of notes using several different sources and subsequent short references might look.

Notes

> 1. Helen Wilkinson, "It's Just a Matter of Time," *Utne Reader* (May/June 1995): 66-67.

2. Paul Osterman, "Getting Started," *Wilson Quarterly* (autumn 1994): 46-55.

3. Newt Gingrich, "America and the Third Wave Information Age," in *To Renew America* (New York: HarperCollins, 1995), 51-61.

4. Ibid., 54.

5. Wilkinson, 66.

6. Ibid.

7. Ibid., 67.

8. Osterman, 48-49.

9. Gingrich, 60.

Notice that note 4 refers to the Gingrich chapter and notes 6 and 7 refer to Wilkinson's article.

4.4.2   CMS bibliographies. At the end of your project, list alphabetically every source cited or used. This list is usually titled "Works Cited" if it includes only works actually mentioned in the project; it is titled "Bibliography" if it also includes works consulted in preparing the project but not actually cited. Because CMS notes are quite thorough, a Works Cited or Bibliography list may be optional, depending on the assignment: check with your instructor or editor about including such a list. Individual items on a Works Cited or Bibliography list are single spaced, with a double space between items.

A typical **CMS Works Cited/Bibliography entry for an electronic source** is arranged and punctuated just like a printed source with some additions.

- Author and title, arranged and punctuated as if for a printed source.

- Publication information (if available), including city, publisher, and date for books or volume number/date for periodicals, followed by a period and one space.

- A description of the electronic format or computer source (*database online*, CD-ROM, *journal online*, *abstract online*), followed by a period and one space.

- An electronic address or path following the words *Available from*. For World Wide Web sites, give the URL (that is, the address that begins *http*) and follow it with a semicolon and the word *Internet*.

- A date of access for online materials. The date of access can appear either before or after the electronic address. If after, it is separated from that address or path by a semicolon and followed by a period.

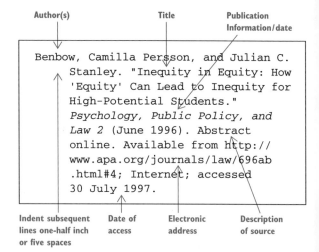

| Author(s) | Title | Publication Information/date |

Benbow, Camilla Persson, and Julian C. Stanley. "Inequity in Equity: How 'Equity' Can Lead to Inequity for High-Potential Students." *Psychology, Public Policy, and Law 2* (June 1996). Abstract online. Available from http://www.apa.org/journals/law/696ab.html#4; Internet; accessed 30 July 1997.

| Indent subsequent lines one-half inch or five spaces | Date of access | Electronic address | Description of source |

There are so many variations to these general entries, however, that you will want to check the CMS Form Directory below for the correct format of any unusual entry.

When an author has more than one work on the list, those works are listed alphabetically under the author's name using this form.

Altick, Richard D. *The Shows of London.* Cambridge: Belknap-Harvard University Press, 1978.

———. *Victorian People and Ideas.* New York: Norton, 1973.

———. *Victorian Studies in Scarlet.* New York: Norton, 1977.

4.4.3   CMS form directory.   In this section, you will find the CMS notes and bibliography forms for several types of electronically accessed sources. The numbered items in the list are the sample note forms; the matching bibliography entries appear immediately after.

CMS Format Index

4.4.3.1.   Computer software

4.4.3.2.   Electronic sources

4.4.3.3.   WWW—book online

4.4.3.4.   WWW—article online

4.4.3.5.   Email

4.4.3.1   Computer Software—CMS

        17. Visual FoxPro Ver. 6.0,
    Microsoft, Seattle, Wash.

    Visual FoxPro Ver. 6.0. Microsoft,
        Seattle, Wash.

4.4.3.2.   Electronic   Sources—CMS   The standards for electronic documentation are in flux. CMS follows the style recommended by the International Standards Organization (ISO). But many issues remain unresolved as new sources and formats evolve. In *The Chicago Manual of Style* (14th ed.), the examples of notes for electronic sources generally include three features: a description of the computer source in brackets, such as *[electronic bulletin board]* or *[Web site]*; the date the material was accessed, updated, or cited *[cited 28 May 1996]*; and an electronic address, following the words *available from*. Models 4.4.3.1 through 4.4.3.5 below follow these recommendations as modified in Kate L. Turabian's *Manual of Style for Writers of Term Papers, Theses, and Dissertations* (6th ed., 1996). The resulting citations are quite complex. Some simplification may be in order, or you may wish to consult Section 4.1 on Columbia Style for online sources.

        18. Sylvia Atore Alva,
    "Differential Patterns of Achievement
    Among Asian-American Adolescents,"

Journal of Youth and Adolescence 22
(1993): 407-23, *ProQuest General
Periodicals* [CD-ROM], UMI-ProQuest,
June 1994.

Alva, Sylvia Atore. "Differential
    Patterns of Achievement Among
    Asian-American Adolescents,"
    Journal of Youth and Adolescence 22
    (1993): 407-23. *ProQuest General
    Periodicals*. CD-ROM UMI-ProQuest,
    June 1994.

4.4.3.3.   WWW—Book Online—CMS

19. Amelia E. Barr, *Remember the
Alamo* [book online] (New York: Dodd,
Mead, 1888); available from http://
etext.lib.virginia.edu/cgibin/
browse-mixed?id=BarReme&tag=
public&images=images/modeng&data=/1v1/
Archive/eng-parsed; Internet; cited
12 May 1997.

Barr, Amelia E. *Remember the Alamo*. Book
    online. New York: Dodd, Mead, 1888.
    Available from http://etext
    .lib.virginia.edu/cgibin/browse-
    mixed?id=BarReme&tag=public&
    images=images/modeng&data=/1v1/
    Archive/eng-parsed; Internet; cited
    12 May 1997.

4.4.3.4.   WWW—Article Online—CMS

20. Paul Skowronek, "Left and Right
for Rights," *Trincoll Journal,* 13 March
1997 [journal online]; available from
http://www.trincoll.edu/~tj/tj03.13.97/
articles/comm2.html; Internet; accessed
23 July 1997.

Skowronek, Paul. "Left and Right for
    Rights." *Trincoll Journal,* 13 March
    1997. Journal online. Available
    from http://www.trincoll.edu/
    ~tj/tj03.13.97/articles/comm2.html;
    Internet; accessed 23 July 1997.

4.4.3.5.   Email—CMS

```
    21. Robert D. Royer, "Re: Are We in
a State of NOMAIL?" Email to author, 22
July 1997.

Royer, Robert D. "Re: Are We in a State
        of NOMAIL?" Email to author, 22
        July 1997.
```

CBE Style

Disciplines that study the physical world—physics, chemistry, biology—are called the natural sciences; disciplines that examine (and produce) technologies are described as the applied sciences. Writing in these fields is specialized, and no survey of all forms of documentation can be provided here. For more information about writing in the following fields, we suggest that you consult one of these style manuals.

- **Chemistry:** *The ACS Style Guide: A Manual for Authors and Editors,* 2nd edition (1997)—American Chemical Society
- **Geology:** *Suggestions to Authors of Reports of the United States Geological Survey,* 7th edition (1991)—U.S. Geological Survey
- **Mathematics:** *A Manual for Authors of Mathematical Papers,* revised edition (1990)—American Mathematical Society
- **Medicine:** *American Medical Association Manual of Style,* 9th edition (1997)
- **Physics:** *AIP Style Manual,* 4th edition (1990)—American Institute of Physics

A highly influential manual for scientific writing is *Scientific Style and Format: The CBE Manual for Authors, Editors, and Publishers* (6th edition, 1994). In this latest edition of *The CBE Manual,* the Council of Biology Editors advocates a common style for international science but also recognizes important differences between disciplines and even countries.

CBE style itself includes the choice of two major methods of documenting sources used in research: a *name-year* system that resembles APA style and a *citation-sequence* system that lists sources in the order of their use. In this section, we briefly describe this second system.

Citing Electronic Sources in the Natural and Applied Sciences.   CBE documentation covers many electronic sources but it does not deal specifically with Web sites and other online environments. When citing such items, you may want to use the documentation style recommended by the *Columbia Guide to Online Style;* it was developed explicitly for newer research situations. Columbia Online Style (COS) for scientific papers, described on pages 156 through 167, is especially adaptable to CBE-style name-year citations. Consult your instructor about using Columbia style for electronic and computerized sources.

(Step 1) Where a citation is needed in the text of a project, insert either a raised number (the preferred form) or a number in parentheses. Citations should appear immediately after the word or phrase to which they are related, and they are numbered in the order you use them.

    Oncologists[1] are aware of trends in
    cancer mortality[2].
    Oncologists(1) are aware of trends in
    cancer mortality(2).

Source 1 thus becomes the first item on the References list, source 2 the second item, and so on.

    1. Devesa SS, Silverman DT. Cancer
       incidence and mortality trends in the

```
    United States: 1935-74. J Natl Cancer
    Inst 1978; 60:545-571.
 2. Goodfield J. The siege of cancer. New
    York: Dell; 1978. 240 p.
```

You can refer to more than one source in a single note, with the numbers separated by a dash if they are in sequence and by commas if out of sequence.

IN SEQUENCE

```
Cancer treatment[2-3] has changed over the
decades. But Rettig[4] shows that the
politics of cancer research remains
constant.
```

OUT OF SEQUENCE

```
Cancer treatment[2,5] has changed over
the decades. But Rettig[4] shows that the
politics of cancer research remains
constant.
```

If you cite a source again later in the project, refer to it by its original number.

```
Great strides have occurred in
epidemiological methods[5] despite the
political problems in maintaining
research support and funding described
by Rettig[4].
```

(Step 2) In a separate list at the end of the text, list the sources you used in the order they occurred.   These sources are numbered: source 1 in the project would be the first source on the References list, source 2 the second item, and so on. Notice, then, that this References list is *not* alphabetical. The first few entries on a CBE list might look like this.

Subsequent lines begin   **"References"**   **All items**
under first words of first line   **centered**   **double spaced**

A typical **CBE citation-sequence–style References entry for an electronic item** includes the basic information provided for a print document (author, title, publication information, page numbers) with the following
additions.

- Electronic medium, identified between brackets. For
  books and monographs, this information comes after
  the title [*monograph on-line*]; for periodicals, it follows
  the name of the journal [*serial on-line*].

- Availability statement, following the publication information or page numbers.

- Date of access, if helpful in identifying what version
  of an electronic text was consulted.

Electronic medium

```
9. Dewitt R. Vagueness, semantics, and
   the language of thought. PSYCHE
   [serial on-line] 1993 July; 1(1).
   Available from: ftp.lib.ncsu.edu via
   the INTERNET. Accessed 1995 Apr 26.
```

Availability statement   **Date of access**

There are so many variations to these basic entries,
however, that you will certainly want to check the *CBE
Manual* when you do a major CBE-style paper.

GLOSSARY

Address.   The route or path followed to access a specific file online. See also *file*, *URL*.

American Standard Code for Information Interchange. See *ASCII*.

Anchor.   Usually refers to a linked designation in a hypertext document. See also *HTTP*, *hypertext*, *link*.

ASCII.   American Standard Code for Information Interchange. A seven-bit code that assigns numbers from 0 to 127 to the English character set; used by many Internet and computer applications to represent text, allowing the transfer of data between applications and platforms. See also *ISO Latin 1*.

Asynchronous.   In Internet communication, refers to electronic mail and other communications not dependent on timing. See also *synchronous*.

BBS.   Bulletin board service. A service that provides dial-in access to remote users, enabling them to obtain files and information and to communicate with other users. Many BBSs also offer varying levels of Internet access to subscribers.

Bitnet.   Because It's Time Network. A wide-area network system for transferring messages. See also *usenet*, *newsgroup*.

Bookmarks.   Called "favorites" in some browsers, bookmarks are a way of marking a specific file, online address, or location within a file for later retrieval. Many Internet browsers include bookmarks files that can be added to and customized by the user.

Boolean operators.   Search terms based on Boolean logic that allow a user to limit and define search criteria. The most commonly used Boolean operators are *and*, *or*, and *not*. See also *keywords*, *search engine*.

Browser.   Software that allows users to access the World Wide Web and move through hypertext links. Some browsers, such as *Lynx*, offer text-only versions of Web pages, while browsers such as Netscape *Navigator* and *Internet Explorer* use graphical interfaces and point-and-click technology. See also *GUI*, *hypertext*, *WWW*.

Bulletin Board Service.   See *BBS*.

CD-ROM. Compact disc, read-only memory. An optical storage device designed to hold large amounts of information on a small round disc. Most CD-ROMs are read-only, which means that files cannot be written to them by users.

Chat rooms. Virtual "rooms" in which multiple users communicate with each other in real time, usually by inputting text on a keyboard.

Client program. A software program, installed on a host computer or on a user's computer, that facilitates certain protocols. Client programs are available for various platforms for FTP, Gopher, Telnet, email, synchronous communications, and a wide array of other common online applications. See also *PPP, shell account.*

Command-line interface. A means of communicating with a computer that requires the user to input a command at a prompt. Internet shell accounts commonly use command-line interfaces. DOS is a personal computer operating system that uses a command-line interface. See also *GUI.*

Compression. A means of transferring and storing data that requires fewer bytes than the original. Commonly used file compression formats include zip, arc, mpeg, jpeg, and gif. See also *GIF, JPEG, MPEG.*

Cyberspace. A term coined by William Gibson in his cyberpunk novel *Neuromancer* to refer to the entire online world, the computerized space in which programs, files, and communications take place. In common usage, *cyberspace* has come to refer to the Internet.

Database. A collection of data or files usually containing common fields or data records which can be organized and manipulated for use in various ways.

Directory. An organizational structure for maintaining files on a computer, similar to a file folder containing individual documents.

Disk/diskette. Various forms of media designed for storage of electronic data, including floppy diskettes (usually contained in a $3\frac{1}{2}$" square plastic case), hard disks, and CD-ROMs.

Disk operating system. See *DOS.*

DNS. Domain name server. The host computer that provides storage and access to files for a particular domain name. See also *domain name, host.*

Domain name. The unique address assigned to an individual site or IP address, such as www.whitehouse.gov. Most

URLs include a domain name followed by the names of any directories and the name of a file. See also *URL*.

Domain name server.   See *DNS*.

DOS.   Disk operating system. Any one of a number of operating systems that controls communication between input, storage, and output devices. Common disk operating systems used by personal computers include MS-DOS, IBM-DOS, and OS/2. Other operating systems include Mac OS (for Macintosh computers), Windows, UNIX, and VMS.

Download.   The act of moving a file from a host or server directory to a local storage medium such as a diskette or hard drive.

Electronic mail.   See *email*.

Email.   Electronic mail. Messages transmitted on the Internet or through other networked systems, generally using modems and telephone lines or some kind of cabling connection, to other users of the system. On most systems, messages are received almost instantaneously and can be read and replied to entirely online.

FAQ.   Frequently asked questions. A FAQ file provides information about a newsgroup, listserv, or other online service or application, including details of membership, discussion topics, and rules or netiquette guidelines.

File.   A single program, document, image, or element with a discrete name and location.

File extension.   Letters or other information appended to a file name, most often used to designate the type of file. For example, the file *document.wpd* identifies a file named *document* in *WordPerfect* document (wpd) format. DOS allows for only three-letter file extensions; some operating systems allow for more. Other commonly used file extensions include .txt (text), .gif (graphics interchange format), .htm or .html (HyperText Markup Language file), and .exe (executable file, or program file).

File transfer protocol.   See *FTP*.

Footer.   Similar to headers in word-processed documents, a means of automatically placing information, such as a copyright notice or page number, at the bottom of each page, usually below the page margin. See also *header*.

Frame.   On World Wide Web sites, frames are designated HTML elements that allow certain information to be retained on screen in the browser window while other WWW pages are accessed within the frame's borders.

FTP. File transfer protocol. A means of transferring files between remote machines or locations on a network.

GIF. Graphics interchange format. A proprietary graphics format that uses file compression to transmit and store graphics. See also *JPEG*, *MPEG*.

Gopher. A menu-driven system for organizing and accessing remote files and programs on the Internet.

Graphical user interface. See *GUI*.

Graphics interchange format. See *GIF*.

GUI Graphical user interface. A computer interface that allows the use of a mouse or other pointing device, rather than a keyboard, to input commands. Both Windows and Macintosh operating systems use graphical user interfaces. See also *command-line interface*.

Header. In word-processed documents, headers may contain information about a document such as the author's last name and the page number. They are usually placed one-half inch from the top of each page. In HTML documents, the term "header" is often used to designate codes that allow the author to include headings (which see) of various sizes in order to aid the reader in finding information on a page or site. See also *footer*.

Heading. Used in documents to separate sections of text and to designate relationships between sections.

Host. A computer that allows one or more remote users to share programs and files. The host computer is the server that provides personal computer users with access to the Internet and to various programs, such as FTP clients or email editors, that reside on the host computer. See also *network*.

HTML. HyperText Markup Language. A scripting language used to create World Wide Web documents; it allows the author to include links and other hypertext features. See also *hypertext*.

HTTP. HyperText Transfer Protocol. The process by which hypertext files (WWW pages) are transferred between remote computers on the Internet. See also *hypertext, protocol*.

Hypertext. "Hot spots" (designated text, graphics, or icons) that the user selects to automatically access or open linked information elsewhere, either within the same document or file or in other documents or files. In nongraphical interfaces, such as *Lynx* browsers, the tab key is often used to move between links, and the enter key may be used in place of clicking a mouse button to follow the link. See also *HTML*.

HyperText Markup Language.   See *HTML*.

HyperText Transfer Protocol.   See *HTTP*.

Internet.   An international network of computers originally designed by the U.S. Department of Defense to ensure communication abilities in the event of a catastrophe. The Internet today connects millions of individual users, universities, governments, businesses, and organizations, using telephone lines, fiber-optic cabling, and other means of connecting computer users to host machines and host machines to each other. See also *network*, *WWW*.

Internet Protocol.   See *IP*.

Internet Relay Chat.   See *IRC*.

Internet service provider.   See *ISP*.

IP.   The means by which packets of information are routed and transmitted between host computers on the Internet.

IP address.   Internet protocol address. The numeric designation for a specific route to a location or host on the Internet.

IRC.   Internet Relay Chat. A real-time synchronous communication site on the Internet that allows multiple users to log in at the same time, connect to various "rooms" called chat rooms organized around topics of mutual interest, and "talk" to each other by inputting text on a keyboard.

ISO Latin 1.   Developed by the International Standards Organization; similar to ASCII code. However, unlike ASCII, ISO Latin 1 allows for the representation of international characters as well as the English character set. See also *ASCII*.

ISP.   Internet service provider. A service that allows users to connect to the Internet, often by dial-in connections or by direct lines, as in a networked computer system.

Java   A powerful programming language that can be run on machines using a variety of operating systems, allowing portability across platforms.

Joint Photographic Experts Group.   See *JPEG*.

JPEG.   Also known as JPG. Joint Photographic Experts Group. A method of file compression used for transmission and storage of color graphics. See also *GIF*, *MPEG*.

JPG.   See *JPEG*.

Keywords. Terms used to search documents or files with any of a variety of search protocols. Many electronic library catalogs allow keyword searches in addition to author, title, and subject searches. On the WWW, search engines often support keyword searches of titles or entire files. See also *Boolean operators*.

Link. Usually, a connection between files or between different locations in a single file. In a hypertext document, a link is a "hot spot" that connects the reader to another location. See also *hypertext*.

Listserv. A program that allows email messages sent to a designated address to be automatically sent to all subscribers to the list. Many people use *listserv* as a generic term to refer to all types of Internet mailing lists.

Modem. Modulator/demodulator. A hardware device that converts data from analog signals (used by voice lines) to digital signals (used by computers), or from digital to analog signals, thus allowing transmission of electronic files via telephone lines.

MOO. MUD, object-oriented. A form of MUD, used for role-playing games, synchronous conferencing, and distance education applications. See also *MUD*.

Motion Pictures Expert Group. See *MPEG*.

MPEG. Also MPG. Motion Pictures Expert Group. A file compression format used for storage and transfer of audio and video files. See also *GIF, JPEG*.

MPG. See *MPEG*.

MUD. Multi-User Dungeon, or Dimension. An interactive site for multiple users on the Internet. See also *MOO*.

Multimedia. Computer applications that integrate text, graphics, and audio and visual elements.

Netiquette. Network etiquette. Guidelines for appropriate online behavior.

Network. Two or more computers or computer systems linked together, using cables, telephone lines, or other devices, allowing them to share programs, files and other information, or peripheral devices such as printers.

Newsgroup. An electronic discussion group organized around a specific topic.

Online. The state of being connected with or to a computer or a network.

Operating system. See *DOS*.

OS.   Operating system. See *DOS*.

Page.   On the WWW, a document or file with a single URL, regardless of its length. See also *site*.

Path.   The route taken through the host computer directory structure to access a specific file or program.

PDF.   Portable document format. PDF files retain all formatting features designed for print, yet they can be exchanged electronically.

Platform.   Usually, the designation of the specific operating system used by a computer, for example, DOS, Windows, Windows 95 or 98, Macintosh, and UNIX. See also *DOS*.

Plug-in.   A software application used to extend the capabilities of WWW browsers.

Point-to-point protocol.   See *PPP*.

PPP.   Point-to-point protocol. A means of accessing the Internet using dial-in connections that allow the use of client programs residing on the user's personal computer. See also *shell account*.

Prompt.   In a command-line interface, a word, symbol (such as a question mark), or other indicator that the computer is waiting for input from the user. See also *command-line interface*.

Protocol.   A set of rules for performing various tasks on the Internet. Common protocols include file transfer protocol (FTP), HyperText Transfer Protocol (HTTP), Gopher protocols, and telnet protocols.

Search engine.   A program that supports keyword searches and, usually, the use of Boolean operators. Some search engines cover only specific sites or types of files; others will search the entire Internet. See also *Boolean operators*, *keywords*.

Server.   A computer, or host machine, which allocates resources and allows sharing of information between various computers on a network.

Shell account.   An account that allows the user to directly access files and programs residing on the server, usually through a command-line interface. See also *command-line interface*, *PPP*.

Site.   On the Internet, a specific domain or Internet address. WWW pages are often referred to as Web sites. A Web site may also consist of a collection of Web pages that comprise a whole body of work, usually with a single index page or file linked to additional pages within the site. See also *page*.

Software. Usually, a computer program that instructs the operating system to perform certain actions to input, retrieve, manipulate, process, output, or store data. Software controls the operating environment and provides an interface for the user to communicate with the computer in various ways.

Synchronous. Describes communication or commands that follow each other in succession. Internet chat rooms and MUDs are synchronous communication sites. See also *chat rooms*, *MUD*.

Tags. Commands, enclosed within angle brackets 〈 〉, used in HyperText Markup Language to designate various hypertextual features. See also *HTML*.

TCP/IP. Transmission Control Protocol/Internet Protocol. A protocol developed by the U.S. Department of Defense, establishing rules for transmission of data between remote computers.

Telnet. An Internet protocol that allows remote access to machines and programs on another computer. Telnet sites may require the user to have an account on the host machine; many telnet sites also allow "guest" accounts.

Transmission Control Protocol/Internet Protocol. See *TCP/IP*.

Uniform resource locator. See *URL*.

UNIX. A language, used by many Internet host machines, which supports multiple users and multitasking.

Upload. The act of transferring a file from a local computer or disk to a remote server or location.

URL. Uniform resource locator. The Internet address used by browser software to connect to sites on the World Wide Web. The URL usually includes a designation of the protocol, a domain name, directories, and a file name.

Usenet. A world-wide network, or BBS (which see), containing thousands of discussion forums called "newsgroups." See also *newsgroup*.

World Wide Web. See *WWW*.

WWW. World Wide Web; also known as the Web. A user-friendly system of organizing documents and files on the Internet, generally accessed using a browser. See also *HTTP*, *Internet*.

INDEX